Mission Incomprehensible

Multilingual Matters

Alsatian Acts of Identity
  LILIANE M. VASSBERG
Attitudes and Language
  COLIN BAKER
Breaking the Boundaries
  EUAN REID and HANS H. REICH (eds)
Called unto Liberty
  COLIN H. WILLIAMS
Citizens of This Country: The Asian British
  MARY STOPES-ROE and RAYMOND COCHRANE
Continuing to Think: The British Asian Girl
  BARRIE WADE and PAMELA SOUTER
Coping with Two Cultures
  PAUL A. S. GHUMAN
European Models of Bilingual Education
  HUGO BAETENS BEARDSMORE (ed.)
Immigrant Languages in Europe
  GUUS EXTRA and LUDO VERHOEVEN (eds)
Language Education for Intercultural Communication
  D. AGER, G. MUSKENS and S. WRIGHT (eds)
Linguistic and Communicative Competence
  CHRISTINA BRATT-PAULSTON
Linguistic Minorities, Society and Territory
  COLIN H. WILLIAMS (ed.)
One Europe - 100 Nations
  ROY N. PEDERSEN

Please contact us for the latest book information:
Multilingual Matters Ltd, Frankfurt Lodge, Clevedon Hall,
Victoria Road, Clevedon, Avon BS21 7SJ, England

Mission Incomprehensible

Roy D. Ingleton

MULTILINGUAL MATTERS LTD
Clevedon • Philadelphia • Adelaide

Library of Congress Cataloging in Publication Data

Ingleton, Roy D.
Mission Incomprehensible: The Linguistic Barrier to Effective Police Cooperation
in Europe/Roy D. Ingleton
Includes bibliographical references and index
1. Police–European Economic Community countries. 2. Police–European
Economic Community countries–International Cooperation. 3. European
Economic Community countries–Languages–Political aspects. 4. Language
planning–European Economic Community countries. I. Title.
HV8194.5.A2137   1994
363.2'094–dc20   93-29933

British Library Cataloguing in Publication Data

A CIP catalogue record for this book is available from the British Library.

ISBN 1-85359-214-5 (hbk)
ISBN 1-85359-213-7 (pbk)

Multilingual Matters Ltd

UK: Frankfurt Lodge, Clevedon Hall, Victoria Road, Clevedon, Avon BS21 7SJ.
USA: 1900 Frost Road, Suite 101, Bristol, PA 19007, USA.
Australia: P.O. Box 6025, 83 Gilles Street, Adelaide, SA 5000, Australia.

Printed and bound in Great Britain by WBC Ltd, Bridgend.

This book is dedicated to Jo

without whose unfailing encouragement, forbearance and support, it would not have been possible to complete it.

Contents

Acknowledgements

My thanks are due to the following, who rendered invaluable assistance in the preparation of this book without which it would not have been possible to write it:

P. Aepli, Commandant de la Police Cantonale, Lausanne, Switzerland
Dr Bielstein, North Rhine-Westphalia Police
Sir Roger Birch, KB, QPM, CBE, Chief Constable, Sussex Police
Dr R Burkhard, Head of the Swiss Federal Police, Berne
Stuart Cameron-Waller, Head of the European Secretariat, Interpol, Lyons
Chief Inspector Della Canning, Devon & Cornwall Constabulary
F. Casteran, Commissaire Principal, Police Nationale, Paris
Paul Condon, MA, Chief Constable of Kent
Herr Dischler, Baden-Württemberg Police, Germany
Christian Duus, Vicerigspolitichef, The Danish Police, Copenhagen
J.P. van Eerde, Korps Rijkspolitie, The Netherlands
Det. Inspector Frank Gallagher, Kent European Liaison Unit
Capt. Ernst Gilgen, Berne Cantonal Police, Switzerland
Inspector John Gledhill, Kent County Constabulary PoliceSpeak Project
Herr Gollong, Rhineland-Palatinate Police, Germany
Yves Guerbette, Commissaire Principal, Police Nationale, Lille
Brigadier H.V. Haynes, South African Police, Pretoria
Joyce Irvine, Co-ordinator, French Language Services, Ontario
Volker Maass, Schleswig-Holstein Police, Germany
Chief Inspector A. McQueen, British Transport Police
Patrice Meyzonnier, Commissaire Principal, Police Nationale, Paris
Herr Schmal, Saarland Police, Germany
Lt Col. Tullio Del Sette, Arma dei Carabinieri, Rome
David Skuli, Commissaire Principal, Police Nationale, Lille
Major L. van der Stock, Ecole Royale Militaire, Brussels
Fred Verdelman, Head of Interpol, The Hague, The Netherlands
Capt. Pierre Vincent, Sûreté du Quebec, Canada
J-J. Willem, Commissaire Divisionnaire, Police Nationale, Strasbourg
The Commissioner, Royal Canadian Mounted Police, Ottawa
The Direktor, Polizei-Führungsakademie, Munster, Germany
The Director-General de la Policia, Madrid
The Director-General, Guardia Civil, Madrid
Exmo. General Comandante Geral, Guarda Nacional Republicana, Lisbon

Introduction

The implementation of the Single European Act during the last decade of the century and beyond, together with the provisions of other agreements such as the Schengen Accord, will effectively demolish the physical barriers between most, if not all, of those countries which belong to the European Community and make it much easier for EC subjects to move from one country to another. Although the vast majority of these will be perfectly ordinary, law-abiding citizens, there is little doubt that this freedom will also be exploited by both petty and major criminals. Paradoxically, however, no such freedom will be extended to police officers who will continue to be required to respect national borders (albeit with a degree of flexibility in some cases).

This open-door policy can only add to the already substantial problems facing modern European police services and might ultimately necessitate the creation of some form of federal European police agency — a European FBI. In the meantime, or what is perhaps a more generally acceptable alternative, the various national forces will be obliged to co-operate and collaborate with each other more and more in order to combat the ever-rising tide of serious crime and other, lesser offences, especially where a common frontier is shared, whether this is of the terrestrial ('green') or the maritime ('blue') variety.

In practice, however, collaboration can be inordinately hampered by the fact that the individual members of these police forces may be native speakers of any one of the nine official Community languages and the national and legal boundaries within which they are required to operate are often coterminous with linguistic boundaries.

The object of this book is therefore to try to determine just what effect the Single Market will have, what problems face the police as a result of the multiplicity of languages spoken in Europe, and what steps have been and are currently being taken to alleviate or overcome these problems.

To avoid 're-inventing the wheel', the published (and a few unpublished) findings of other researchers and writers have been consulted to see to what extent the matter has been addressed by them, a task which proved surprisingly unfruitful. In an effort to find some answers, therefore, a direct

1

approach was made to the various police forces concerned (or thought likely to be concerned), supplemented by personal interviews with authoritative representatives of some of these forces. The Chief Constables of most of the United Kingdom police forces were asked to describe their policies and views, as were the heads of the principal police and gendarmerie forces in the main Member States of the European Community. In addition, a limited survey was conducted among the police forces in other countries where there is a similar problem arising out of the existence of two or more official languages, to act as a form of control sample and to help in the quest for some form of 'best practice'.

Although there are currently 12 countries in the European Community (EC), this book concentrates on just nine of these:

The United Kingdom	Spain
France	Belgium
Germany	The Netherlands
Italy	Denmark
Portugal	

Three countries were excluded, the reasons for this decision being as follows:

Luxembourg: the population of this country is the smallest in the European Community (c. 350,000) and it is no larger than a small county in the United Kingdom. Similarly, the country's two police forces (the Grand Ducale Gendarmerie and the Corps de la Police) have a combined strength of only some 750 — not much more than a good-sized division in most other countries. Its geographical position and history also means that it has peculiar language requirements: the official language is French, the language of commerce and the press is German while a local language, Letzebuergesch, is also spoken. For these reasons it was felt that to include this small, anomalous State would have an undesirable and adverse effect on the reliability of the findings. It was therefore decided to exclude Luxembourg from the survey.

Ireland: with a population of only 3.5 million, this country has the next smallest population in the European Community and a police strength of under 10,000. Its only terrestrial border is shared with another English-speaking province (Ulster) and this, coupled with the nation's island character, mean that it has little direct contact with continental Europe and so it, too, was eliminated from the study.

Greece: this country was excluded because of its essentially 'island' character, having no land border with any other Member State of the European Community. Its language problems were seen to be peculiar to

Greece, given that its land borders are with Albania, Yugoslavia, Bulgaria and Turkey, none of which employ one of the more common European languages. It was therefore decided that to include this country in the survey would be likely to distort the results.

The number of discrete police forces, gendarmeries and other, similar law-enforcement agencies in Europe is legion. It was therefore decided to ignore the many small, municipal forces in continental Europe, most of the Scottish forces and the City of London Police. The former were excluded in view of their limited policing powers and circumscribed involvement in crime matters, the Scottish forces in view of their remoteness from the rest of Europe, and the City of London force in view of the predominance of the Metropolitan Police in the English capital. In addition, all of these are small in size and have a limited jurisdiction.

Three Scottish forces, Strathclyde Police, Lothian and Borders Police and Dumfries and Galloway Police were included however; the first two because of their size and importance, covering as they do Glasgow and Edinburgh respectively, and the latter in view of its very relevant and recent experience resulting from the Lockerbie air crash. Other UK forces surveyed included the British Transport Police and the Dover Harbour Board Police as it was felt that these were very directly involved in the problem and could provide a positive input to the survey.

Methodology

Given that the research population consisted of a fairly discrete and exhaustive number of police forces, it was possible to make use of the entire responding population, rather than employ any randomisation process to extract a meaningful sample. This meant that heavy reliance had to be placed on the data supplied, separating the hard facts from mere opinion in the responses to the questionnaires and the views propounded during personal interviews. Of course, in doing this one has to be alive to the possibility of bias, partisanship, partiality or chauvinism creeping into the responses. However, the accuracy of the sample is greatly enhanced by the fortunately small number of forces unable or unwilling to participate in the survey, or which provided limited or incomplete responses. To provide a measure of security against the possible shortcomings inherent in this method of data extraction, a close watch was kept on areas which conflicted with the other replies, widely divergent responses being treated with great caution and flagged as such. This has, of course, involved a distinct measure of subjectivity on my part which, again, has been indicated where appropriate.

Whilst accepting that generalisations are unreliable and should be avoided, I started with three basic assumptions which I believed could be made with little likelihood of contradiction:

(1) No one policeman can speak all nine languages of the EC;
(2) Some police officers are able to communicate adequately in one or more foreign languages;
(3) Most police officers only speak their native tongue.

Nothing in my research has demonstrated that these assumptions were in any way unjustified.

Areas of Concern

For the sake of convenience and clarity, the problem has been broken down into three main areas of concern:

(1) *Senior officers*: There seems little doubt that existence of a common European language would greatly facilitate discussions concerning international crime and common policing problems between senior police officers and similar policy-makers from different countries .
(2) *Detectives*: Officers who have to investigate crimes or interview suspects and witnesses in other countries are often hampered by their inability to speak the vernacular of the country concerned. The use of interpreters has the effect of filtering the responses made by interviewees and thereby watering down the sort of unconscious feedback on which an experienced interrogator relies.
(3) *General policing*: Where officers working on or near national frontiers do not share a common language or speak the language(s) of the adjacent country/countries, urgent communication with (a) their colleagues across the border and (b) with foreign visitors who may have committed offences, become victims of crime, or who otherwise seek assistance, is greatly inhibited.

Finally, it seemed reasonable to assume that most, if not all, forces affected by this phenomenon have taken or intend to take steps to obviate or alleviate these difficulties. These could be, for example, the recruitment of linguists for certain posts, the allocation of linguistically skilled officers to certain key posts, or the training of some or all their personnel in one or more of the appropriate languages.

The reader will find, in the appropriate chapters of this book, the extent to which these hypotheses were supported by subsequent research and some of the steps taken to remedy the situation. The works of other authors which relate to languages as they affect communication in general and, in particular, the effect which the profusion of languages spoken in the European Community has on effective policing in Europe, are reviewed, with particular emphasis being placed to the following issues:

(i) The languages of Europe, their development and the manner in which they affect communication at the present time, and the extent to which the introduction of the Single European Act will affect such communication.

(ii) The various vehicles of communication and the experience of bi- and multilingual countries (South Africa, Switzerland, Canada) and the research which has been carried out on bi- and multilingualism.

(iii) The implications for the police forces of Europe.

Although much has been written about policing problems in general and, in recent years, a wide variety of books and articles have addressed the problems of '1992', most of these tend to ignore or skate over the question of language and one has to look elsewhere for coverage of this aspect. Analogous to this, most works which appraise languages and language training overlook the police while the many contemporary language awareness programmes seem to be exclusively directed at the businessman, stressing the advantages to be gained if he can speak the language of his foreign customers. Other language books and articles cover the pedagogical aspect or the psychological and other effects of bilingualism. All of these areas have been closely examined for their relevance to the police in Europe.

Having thoroughly reviewed the situation which currently obtains within the various relevant European policing bodies, the book concludes with an analysis of the diverse steps being taken by them (and others) to overcome the problems associated with the use of more than one language.

1 The Background to the Problem

Historical Overview

The problem of establishing communication between speakers of different languages is not new; perhaps the earliest reference appears in the Bible where it is written:

> And they said: Go to, let us build us a city and a tower...lest we be scattered abroad upon the face of the earth. And the Lord said, Behold, the people is one *and they all have one language*...let us go down and there confound their language that they might not understand one another's speech. So the Lord scattered them abroad...

Some observers would have us believe that this Biblical story should be seen as a portent of the dangers inherent in employing a common tongue in order to collaborate with others in the building of a new city (or, in the case in point, a new Community). In fact, as far back as we can trace, Man has always spoken many different languages; if at any time he spoke a single language from which all other languages descended then it has resisted the concerted efforts of numerous scholars to find it.

Most authorities now accept that the languages of the world fall into around 20 family groups. The most important of these, for our purposes, is the Indo-European family which embraces almost all the existing and ancient European languages.

In the course of the centuries which have followed the ill-fated Tower of Babel, a great many languages have evolved and developed, emerged and disappeared. At the end of the twentieth century there are still thousands of languages spoken across the world. The exact number is impossible to determine as it is always difficult to conclude just when a dialect (which the Oxford English Dictionary defines as 'A subordinate variety of a language showing sufficient differences from the standard language in vocabulary, pronunciation or idiom, for it to be considered as distinct') becomes a discrete language. For example, Flemish, spoken in part of Belgium, is the same language as the Dutch spoken in the Netherlands, but cultural and religious distinctions over the centuries have led to the use of separate terms for what is in fact the same language. The further north one goes in the Netherlands, the more the *dialect* diverges from that spoken on the Belgian border, but both remain nonetheless Dutch. Afrikaans, however, although a derivative of Dutch, is sufficiently different from the parent language for it to be considered a discrete language. Similarly, Dutch itself, once a mere Low German (*Plattdeutsch*) dialect, has long since evolved into a definite language. What is difficult to determine is the precise point at which a dialect diverges sufficiently from the basic tongue for it to be regarded as a different language.

Weber (1990) describes language as a means of communication which uses bricks (words) held together by mortar (grammar) to form its structures (meaning). This description undoubtedly owes more than a little to Chomsky's (1979) contention that the sentence is the basic component of language and that, from a few basic sentence types, an infinity of actual sentences can be produced by a series of rules codified as transformational grammar.

Even in what is now Great Britain there have been what has been eloquently described as 'kaleidoscopic changes' and developments over the last two thousand years. Glanville Price (1984) refers to the various invasions and incursions by the Romans and the Germanic tribes of Scandinavia and Northern Europe, all of which left their mark, and relates how Anglo-Saxon and Viking invaders drove the native Celts to the extremities of the country and imposed their own languages on the land.

Prior to the Norman conquest four distinct Germanic dialects could be distinguished in Great Britain: Mercian, Northumbrian, Kentish and West Saxon. Mitchell & Robinson (1964) describe how it was the latter which developed into what we now call Old English, defined as the vernacular Germanic language as recorded before c. AD 1100. The process of language imposition was continued by the Normans, the last of the great linguistic intrusions experienced by this country. The Norman French spoken by King William's followers had a profound and lasting effect on the language of the country; it introduced thousands of new words which merged with the existing form of Old English to create what is known as Middle English (c. 1150–1500). Many of the anomalies created by this merger can still be seen today and this explains why live animals (which were tended by the Anglo-Saxon serfs) still retain their Germanic names (sheep, cow, calf) while the meat which they provide (as eaten by the Norman overlords) is known by a Norman-French nomenclature (mutton, beef, veal) As Jenkins (1980) illustrates, by the end of the sixteenth century Middle English had given way to Modern English — the language of Shakespeare.

Such transformations were not, of course, confined to this country and one may cite the imposition of the French language on the inhabitants of the newly-united France in the sixteenth century as described by Hamers & Blanc (1989). The emergence of French as the language of the courtier and of diplomacy encouraged the French to have what Harzic (1976) refers to as '...*une conviction innée de la supériorité de leur langue*', whilst the Austro-Hungarian influence resulted in German becoming the official language for a large part of Europe.

Whereas in the Middle Ages, it took several generations for a language to change appreciably, today languages are evolving at an unprecedented rate and, as Weber (1990) puts it, 'Never have so many speakers of one language misunderstood, made love to, had convivial drinks with...so many people of another language'.

As the years go by some languages evolve and gain wider acceptance whilst others die out, giving rise to some interesting theories being postulated as to why this phenomenon occurs. Some languages, it is maintained, die because they are taken over by their offspring, such as the Romance languages which supplanted Latin; others die as the result of a 'marriage' or merger (Anglo-Saxon + Norman French = English). A further group dies because there is no one left who speaks the language; the last native Cornish speaker, Dorothy Pentreath, was buried in 1777, her tombstone recording the demise of the language with her. Hughes (1988) tells how the last native Tasmanian speaker, an Aborigine named Trucanini, died on the Australian mainland in 1876, following the expulsion of the last few blacks from the island — an affair in which she played no small part. But in most cases a language simply disappears because the cultures it supported have been absorbed by more powerful and more successful cultures.

Over the past century or so there has been a significant increase in the number of people who can speak one or other of a very select number of languages, most of these speakers having learned it as a second language. A few other languages have grown and this is usually because of a population explosion among its native speakers. But de Swaan (1991) has shown how, in many more cases, the populace have abandoned their mother tongue or simply have not passed it on to their children. As a result, a rapidly increasing number of speakers interact with each other in a dwindling number of languages.

It is estimated that there are about 5,000 languages in existence today but, of these, only a mere 60 or so can boast more than 10 million speakers. Their combined total represents 90% of the world's population. Ten or twelve of these have yet another order of magnitude: they are each spoken by at least 100 million people. Together they account for some 60% of the world's population. Finally, one (or perhaps two) languages count a billion or more speakers: Chinese and (possibly) English.

The Countries of Europe and Their Languages

Crystal (1987) describes how the evolution of languages in Europe has resulted in there being four countries in the European Community which use Latin-based Romance languages (France, Italy, Spain, Portugal), six using a Germanic language (Germany, Great Britain, Ireland, Denmark, Netherlands, Luxembourg), one which combines the two (Belgium) and one where an ancient language is spoken (Greece). Of the Romance languages, Spanish has by far the greatest number of native speakers worldwide, but these are mainly to be found in South and Central America. For this, and for historical reasons (not excluding the influence of Napoleon Bonaparte) French became and remains the dominant Romance language spoken in Europe. On the other hand, although the greatest number of speakers of a Germanic language are to be found in the newly-unified Germany (c. 100 million), the enormous influence of North America on world affairs usually results in English being the most widely-spoken language of this group.

Intercommunication Between Nations

Jean Monnet, the 'Father of the Common Market', was anxious that Western Europe should unite to form a kind of United States of Europe. When the European Economic Community was created by the Treaty of Rome in 1957, it was based on an alliance of just six nations: France, Germany, Italy, and the Benelux countries. The decision to treat all the languages spoken in these countries as official Community languages created few problems, involving as it did only four distinct tongues: French, German, Italian and Dutch. Communication between these countries was not unduly difficult and, in practice usually involved the use of the first two languages, the Italian and Dutch speakers generally accepting the use of these more-common languages.

The question of a common language was not a pressing one in these early days. But with the growth of the Community to 12 involving the use of nine discrete languages, communication has become an enormous problem and an almost insupportable burden. At the institutional level the Community is only able to operate effectively because it employs a whole army of interpreters and translators — at enormous cost. Without the services of these professional linguists (accounting for around a third of all Community employees) the whole bureaucratic machinery would grind to a halt. As Owen & Dynes (1989) have been quick to point out, few commercial firms can contemplate anything like this sort of expenditure and the lack of language skills will be felt particularly acutely in countries such as Great Britain and Ireland which have a poor reputation for acquiring foreign languages.

Despite Monnet's vision of the burgeoning European Community as a sort of 'United States of Europe', where the criminal justice and language fields are concerned any comparison with the United States of America must be regarded as seriously misleading. The official language for the whole of the United States (although not formally acknowledged as such) is English. If one ignores the handful of French or Creole speakers in Louisiana and the growing number of Hispanics in all states, the actual language spoken in all the United States is indeed English and this does not change when one crosses a state border; the official language remains English in all 50 states.

As McKenzie & Gallagher (1989) have demonstrated, although (with the exception of a limited number of federal crimes) most criminal law is enacted by the individual state legislatures and each state has its own criminal justice system, the essential laws and judicial systems throughout the Union differ only in detail. It is true that, in Louisiana (which was a French possession until it was ceded to the USA in 1803) the legal system has remained based on the French model but this may be regarded as an aberration and, on the whole, the differences in legal systems are negligible compared with those which exist in Europe.

Malcolm Anderson (1989) cites the excellent relations which exist between the FBI in the US and the RCMP in Canada to demonstrate that, where there is no language difference, policing and judicial variations can readily be overcome, given goodwill on both sides. Unfortunately this essential goodwill is all too often absent; petty rivalries and jealousies abound and refusal to cooperate is unfortunately all too common, even within the same country. One has only to look more closely at the United States to see that there is frequently fierce competition between the FBI and local police departments, between the City Police and the County Sheriff's Department and so on, especially where there is political kudos to be obtained. In Europe there are numerous examples of lack of cooperation between a country's National Police and its Gendarmerie, between the police in the capital and those in the provinces. These problems can only be magnified where chauvinistic or nationalistic considerations might obtain.

The concept of 'goodwill' was pursued by Catherine Spencer (1989) whose project in applied linguistics revealed that 80% of those interviewed felt that native speakers of English should be more sensitive to the difficulties of non-native speakers, while 60% resented the lack of linguistic skills possessed by native English speakers. A similar number were irritated by the implied assumption that everyone should speak English.

Hamers & Blanc (1989) have made an extensive study of how a country solves its communication problems where it employs many different languages within its boundaries and we may be justified in extrapolating this to the European Community. One method identified is the forcible imposition of a single national language, the solution adopted by the French in 1539 following the Ordonnance de Villers-Coterêts, and by the Spanish *Conquistadores* in South and Central America. A more subtle solution is the use of a language planning scheme, as illustrated by Malaya which has adopted Bahasa Malaysia as the sole official language. On the other hand, the scheme adopted by neighbouring Singapore, which has a similar ethnic mix, makes provision for no less than four official languages under its language plan.

The explosion in air traffic generated an urgent need for speech to be unambiguous and clearly understood by all connected with air traffic control and led to the introduction of 'Airspeak' which has been more than adequately portrayed by Field (1985). It is solely because of the overwhelming importance of the USA in aviation matters that this procedure is based on the English language. In a later chapter we shall see how this concept is being applied to policing through the 'PoliceSpeak' project inaugurated by the Kent County Constabulary.

The Effect of 1992

The implementation of the Single European Act after 31 December 1992 may have eased certain problems of movement and domicile but it in no way alleviates the difficulties associated with national languages.

What matters it how far we go?', his scaly friend replied,
There is another shore you know, upon the other side.
The further off from England, the nearer is to France,
Then turn not pale, beloved snail, but come and join the dance.

The Mock Turtle's song about the whiting and the snail pre-dates the Single European Act by some 130 years but it is no less relevant for all that. It is to be hoped that the coincidences between the Single Market and 'Alice in Wonderland' do not include the Mad Hatter's Tea Party or any of the other manic scenes described by Lewis Carroll (1865) but there is no doubt that Great Britain is moving nearer and nearer to France (and the rest of Continental Europe) — a fact which the opening of the Channel Tunnel can only accelerate.

Jacques Delors, the President of the European Commission is reported to have expressed surprise at the impact of the phrase '1992' since:

> ...it merely signifies the end of the legislative process required to bring the Single European Market into being; nothing more, nothing less. Nothing will change — nothing visible at least — at midnight on 31 December 1992.

Indeed, as Professor Nigel Reeves (1989) has asserted, the Single European Market is already with us and the '1992' date is merely symbolic — a date by which all should be in place. Reeves has also identified the three main barriers which must be demolished: the physical barriers, technical barriers and fiscal barriers, the former having the greatest impact on the police.

However, a further barrier recognised by Reeves, that of language, is another obstacle which, as we shall see, has great significance for many of the inhabitants of Europe, including the police. This barrier will effectively inhibit what has been described by the Chief Constable of Sussex, Sir Roger Birch (1989b), as the 'need to exchange information freely and speedily between nations', given that even internal borders have proved to be an obstacle to effective communication.

At this point it might be politic to pause for a moment and examine the policies of the European Community as they affect this question. The concept of an international community without internal frontiers is not the recent invention of some crazed bureaucrat in Brussels; the Treaty of Rome (Art. 3c) committed members, from the outset, to 'the abolition...of obstacles to the freedom of movement for persons, services and capital'. In the Single European Act of 1986, Ministers agreed to establish, by the end of 1992, 'an area without internal frontiers in which the free movement of goods, persons, services and capital is ensured'. These are the four basic freedoms, the four 'pillars of wisdom' which the Community holds dear.

So far as goods, services and capital are concerned, the goal is either already achieved or well on the way but the abolition of internal frontier controls on people has proved a less tractable problem. It is not insoluble, however; the Anglo-Irish Free Travel Area operates very smoothly despite the grave terrorist threat. The Nordic countries have long been parties to an agreement which eliminates frontier controls between them and which is highly popular with their respective populations.

Despite the very evident difficulties, the commitment of the Community's Member States and institutions, as described by the European Commission itself (1985) is unequivocal:

It is the physical barriers at the customs posts, the immigration controls, the passports, the occasional search of personal baggage which, to the ordinary citizen, are the obvious manifestation of the continued division of the Community.

It is evident, therefore, that there can be no exceptions whatsoever to the decision, enshrined in the Single European Act, to eliminate all such controls, which in practice will mean that all border posts between EC countries must eventually disappear.

The most recent prototype for a frontier-free Community is the Schengen agreement signed in 1985 between France, Germany and the Benelux countries, and subsequently subscribed to by Italy, Spain and Portugal, which provides for the total abolition of checks on persons at the common frontiers of the participating countries. But, in fact, little real cooperation will be possible without what Valerie Giscard d'Estaing referred to as '*une espace juridique européen*' — a European legal area — which assumes progress towards some form of codification of Community crimes and, possibly, the setting up of a European police force to tackle international organised crime, together with supranational courts to sit in judgement.

A *lingua franca*

Much thought has been given to the most practical means of overcoming this language barrier. As we have already seen, one method is the imposition or adoption of a common language, a *lingua franca*. Over the centuries, various languages have served as the *lingua franca* of the civilised world — Greek, Latin, French and now, English. If the European Community were to adopt this solution, which language should it use? Leaving aside purely artificial languages (Esperanto, Interlingua, etc.) the choice must obviously lie with one of the nine official EC languages. De Swaan (1991) suggests that the whole constellation of languages may be depicted as a Venn diagram in which English, in the centre, intersects with a dozen supranational languages, the overlaps or intersections representing multilingual speakers.

For this reason, in Europe, one can discount the minority languages of Greek, Danish, Dutch and Portuguese. Similarly, the number of Europeans whose mother tongue is Spanish or Italian is limited, leaving German, French and English as the only significant contenders. One point in favour of English is that it is a combination of both Latin and Teutonic languages; the French student of English quickly finds words and concepts he can recognise. The same applied to his German counterpart, although the words with which he identifies will be different ones. As both German and French have largely remained 'pure', the French student of German finds little correlation with his own language, a situation which applies equally to the German student of French.

Linguistically speaking, there is nothing intrinsic to a language that makes it superior or inferior to another. What decides the fate of a language under attack is the economical, political and technological superiority of the people speaking the incursive language. In other words, brute strength counts much more than cultural superiority. If English is today tending to become the *lingua franca* of the world and not, for example, Hungarian or Malay, it is not because it is better suited to its role in some mysterious way. As Weber (1990) points out, English is paramount because it just happened to be the language of certain people who were historically in the right place at the right time. The growth of English as a global *lingua franca* is an indisputable and inescapable consequence of modern travel and communications.

The imposition of a single Community language is an obvious and, to the British, attractive one — assuming that the language imposed is English! Binyon (1989) has already been suggested that 'the English language looks set to become the undisputed world language in the 1990s', while Canning (1990) illustrates how it pervades the world as the most acceptable common language for use at conferences and for business, that it is dynamic (thus allowing for the creation of new words), that it is the sole (or a major) official language in some 70 countries throughout the world and that it is widely taught in schools in most European countries.

In 1991 the *Daily Mail* conducted a short-lived campaign for just this solution on the grounds that English is the nearest thing the world has to a universal language. A subsequent article by Bell & Norris (1991) in the same newspaper reported widespread support for such an initiative throughout Europe, quoting a Greek businessman as voicing what many British people have long suspected: 'English is the common language, except in certain chauvinist parts of France where, although they can speak English, they refuse to'. Not surprisingly, the French are violently opposed to the prospect and President Mitterrand, following the francophonic tradition of his predecessor, Charles de Gaulle, is reported by Tomlins (1991) as having warned his country's civil servants that, if they spoke a foreign language at an international meeting, they would face dismissal.

The idea of using English as the common Community language is doubtless based on the fact that it is the mother tongue of some 350 million people throughout the world and is spoken by many millions more as their second language. This compares with the figures quoted by Crystal (1987) of 250 million Spanish Speakers, 100 million German and a mere 70 million French native speakers.

Such is the potency of the English language that, according to the Director of Amsterdam's Free University Language Centre, 89% of Dutch firms perceive a need for English in their trading activities, an increase of 25% since 1978. This compares with 64% who felt a need for German and 53% for French.

This is not to suggest that everyone will readily accept English as the dominant language of Europe. In an unresolved situation, any language group will jealously try to prevent other groups from achieving dominance as this would mean *its* members having to learn the other language rather than being able to profit from others learning theirs. Language is no longer taken for granted but is increasingly seen as a symbol, a cherished and historical treasure. Not all thinking people therefore slavishly follow the 'English Rules' notion.

The unification of Germany, coupled with its economic might, gives credence to the concept of German as a primary European language. It is the mother tongue of more Europeans than any other and, for historical and geographical reasons, the second language for many inhabitants of Eastern Europe . To a German, *Sprache ist Macht* — language is power!, but it is an undeniable fact that, outside Europe, German is used in very few locations.

Despite the tenacity with which its citizens adhere to their native tongue to the exclusion of any other, and strenuously repel the intrusion of any foreign terms, no claim by France for its language to be adopted throughout Europe could be seriously entertained. Although some French is spoken by quite a number of Europeans whose mother tongue is another Romance language (Spanish, Italian, Portuguese, etc.), its use is far from common in the more northern parts of Europe.

There is a strong body of opinion which feels that the robustness of the European states and the firmly-rooted use of their own languages makes it unlikely that there will be any language unification. Jealousy between the major language groups (especially French and German) will ultimately prevent any one tongue from becoming the official language of the European Community. Other bodies and individuals seek to promote one of the artificial languages, such as Esperanto or Interlingua, as the common language for Europe. These are seen as being free from any nationalistic overtones, although the Latin base of at least the latter creation is likely to militate against it amongst speakers of the Teutonic languages of Europe.

Cross-border Bilingualism

The principal alternative to the use of a common language is the learning of one or more of the other languages of, in this case, the Community. Van Deth (1989) foresees the development and expansion of new *espaces linguis-*

tiques — areas in which bilateral exchanges on a European level will increasingly bring together executives and experts at middle management level. He asserts that, for such people, the English language does not offer any particular advantage whereas the use of the language of their opposite number does. For some Europeans there is much more to be gained from speaking the language of their neighbour than using a language which is foreign to both parties, and van Deth also foresees the development of 'neighbourly solidarity' between the Latin countries on the one hand and the Northern countries on the other, resulting in a wider use of German, Spanish and French as the corollary of European development. As will be seen in subsequent chapters, this solution is already being adopted by a number of European police forces, notably those in France and Germany.

For the continental European, the decision as to which language to study is largely influenced by (a) the dominance of English and (b) the language(s) of his near neighbours. Thus, one would expect the Dane and the Dutchman to learn German, the Portuguese to learn Spanish, the Spaniard Portuguese or French, etc. For a German, however, the choice is not so clear as his EC neighbours may speak French, Dutch or Danish, while the languages of his non-EC *Nachbaren* include Polish, Czech and Slovak in addition to several nearly-incomprehensible versions of the German language such as those spoken in parts of Austria and Switzerland.

The British language student will have to decide whether he should learn the language of one of the country's near neighbours such as French or Dutch, or look further afield to those countries with which he is most likely to have dealings. Pandit (1989) suggests that the speakers of the central language in a floral model (or Venn diagram) of language unification do not gain much by learning a second language themselves, but profit when peripheral language speakers learn their language. If this is indeed the case, there is a very good excuse for the Briton's perceived reluctance to learn any other language.

However, if the British are going to learn a foreign language they must decide which foreign language should be taught in their schools and, by extension, to adults. Should this be French, German, Spanish, or indeed one of the ethnic minority languages such as Punjabi, Gujarati, Urdu, etc.? This question is one which is taxing several British police forces, especially in those areas where there is a high level of ethnic settlement.

The predominance of French language teaching in schools has been fully discussed elsewhere and Westgate (1989) quotes statistics to show that, in 1986, 64.4% of all modern language 'A' level candidates took French. Of the language options offered by schools in 1982, 90% offered French against 21% German and only 4% Spanish. Failing the adoption of English as the common European language, or at least tacit acceptance of its universal use, the British will have to give much more serious consideration to the learning of another language or languages.

There is a widespread belief, largely shared by the British themselves, that the inhabitants of the United Kingdom are unable or unwilling to learn other languages. This conviction belies the truth, however; as Cross (1991) points out, history shows that, in the past, members of the Colonial Service (including the Colonial Police) were very good at languages. Indeed, law and order depended on it and officers regarded it as an insult to be spoken to in English as this indicated that the person addressing them presumed they had not bothered to learn the vernacular. And it must be remembered that the colonial languages concerned (Malayan, Hindi, Urdu, Chinese, Swahili, etc.) are infinitely more difficult to learn than European ones.

So far as the police service is concerned, to overcome this lacuna in language skills it is proposed that there is firstly, a need to identify multi-lingual officers and secondly, to train suitable members of the force.

Language Acquisition

The usual objective in learning a foreign language is to improve communication with and to get to know people of a different culture. It is also clear that it is the differences between one form of speech and another which inhibit mutual understanding and, equally clearly, that where such differences exist, the decisive level of proficiency is that which allows one to overcome the lack of intelligibility between the two languages concerned. This raises the question of bilingualism (or multilingualism) — whatever this much-abused term implies. Hamers (1981) defines bilingualism as the psychological state of an individual who has access to more than one linguistic code as a means of social communication. Not all other writers are able to agree on precisely what the term means; it is commonly taken to mean a near-native control of two languages but Macnamara (1967) proposes 'anyone who possesses a minimum competence in one of the four language skills' (listening, speaking, reading, writing). True bilingualism is not, however, without its own problems such as loss of national and cultural identity and these are covered in depth by Munro (1987) in her work on bilinguals in Wales.

In the absence of an acceptable degree of competence in a common language or a suitable foreign tongue, one must give consideration to the teaching of languages and a suitable system by which they might be learnt. Some countries in the European Community already boast an enviable expertise in this respect but Great Britain and certain other countries lag far behind.

There is no shortage of literature on the subject of foreign language teaching/learning and most works stress the pressing need for the British to acquire foreign languages, especially those who will have dealings with, or are likely to come into contact with foreign nationals. It is not too fanciful to assert that, in the near future, only those who are able to make their skills and knowledge readily available to countries outside their own will be successful, and that there is a need for at least two foreign languages to be taught in all schools. This viewpoint is supported by the widely-held contention that we must grasp the simple truth that knowledge of foreign languages is not an end to itself but an essential skill for anyone seeking to make their mark in any discipline at international level. To learn another language is to acquire a valuable instrument in influencing and under-standing others: to learn a language is to learn how others think.

Once one accepts the need to acquire foreign languages, the question arises 'whom do we train?'. To address the question of language teaching in schools is all very well but must obviously be seen as a long-term solution. By the time today's scholars are ready to enter the police service we shall be into the next century and so, where there has been a lack of suitable tuition in the schools, we must look for more immediate solutions. If the police need linguists, should the service train its personnel to be linguists, or should it employ linguists as police officers? This question has been addressed by Wickland (1989) (in the context of executives v. linguists) who points out that, while it takes about five years to develop a good manager, it takes about three months for anyone of this intellectual calibre to learn (say) German to an effective level. Moreover, it is quicker to determine whether a subject has the capacity to learn a language than it is to determine whether he/she has executive/management potential.

Wickland readily accepts that not everyone can acquire another language with equal facility and extensive research has already been made into this subject. Hamers & Blanc (1989) point to the differences in aptitude for language learning and to variations in memory retention. Littlewood (1984) has pursued this aspect further, demonstrating how the speech of language learners varies according to the prevalent situation and how they adopt non-linguistic strategies to compensate for the gaps in their linguistic ability. He also makes the very valid point that research into second language acquisition is a comparatively new field and that there are still considerable gaps in our knowledge.

Nevertheless, teaching methods have demonstrably evolved over the years. The most widely known method, *Grammar–Translation*, traditionally used in the learning of the Classics, dates from the last century and imparts good reading skills but poor oral fluency — a skill which has little value where dead languages are concerned. Although this method is still used by some teachers, the turn of the century saw the introduction of the *direct method* in which the emphasis is on speech, translation being seen as positively harmful since it provokes Mother tongue interference. Unlike the grammar-translation method, this system provides good oral fluency but fails to impart any grammatical awareness, making it difficult for learners to progress on their own.

In the 1950s and 1960s the *audio-lingual* method emerged, resulting in language laboratories springing up everywhere and seen as the panacea for all language learning ills. The audio-lingual method places great emphasis on listening, speaking, reading and writing (in that order) but, over the years, it has become apparent that, in practice, there is a serious problem with 'withdrawal of meaning' owing to insufficient contextualisation — learners are able to chant their drills successfully but lack understanding of what they are saying. The method has now been largely discredited by, amongst others, the eminent American linguist, Chomsky, as being based on untenable views and lacking in scientific principles.

The most recent innovation has been LSP (Languages for Specific Purposes) which makes no attempt to teach the *whole* language, but concentrates on specific areas of interest to the student. We shall be returning to this concept later when we look at the 'PoliceSpeak' project.

If the police in Europe accept that there is a need to train their officers to speak another language (or languages), which should it be? This question has been addressed in general terms above and, so far as Great Britain is concerned, it seems appropriate, given the geographical location of this country, to continue to support the learning of French, with German as second choice in view of its economic importance and size.

Against this one must bear in mind James's (1978) 'inter-language' contrasts, in which he attempts to give a score to five major European languages according to a scale of difficulty, the higher the score, the greater the distance from English (see Table 1.1). In the table, *phonological* refers to the sound of the spoken word, *grammatical* describes the syntax and grammar structure, *lexical* indicates the use of similar words and phrases, *spelling* is self-explanatory while *orthographic* concerns the representation of verbal sounds by literal symbols (e.g. letters or characters).

Once it has been decided which language(s) is/are to be taught and they have embarked on a suitable course of training, training officers will find it necessary to assess the degree of absorption and test levels of competence. There is no shortage of advice here; Baker (1989) proposes a couple of models which make explicit certain principles which operate in language testing and goes on to examine what the tests are intended to achieve. For

Table 1.1

	French	German	Italian	Russian	Spanish
Phonological	4	2	1	3	2
Grammatical	2	3	2	3	2
Lexical	1	2	1	4	1
Spelling	4	2	1	2	1
Orthographic	1	1	1	4	1
Totals	12	10	6	16	7

their part, Brumfit & Roberts (1983) specify four types of test and suggest certain methods to be adopted including dictation (to measure total language proficiency), Cloze tests (insertion of missing words) and criterion-referenced tests (simulating real-life situations).

Before leaving the question of language skills, it is interesting to note that, sometimes, even those whom the British would regard as having an excellent command of languages have misgivings about their ability. As an example, Koster (1991) suggests that, where a fluent English-speaking Dutchman might simply say, 'I don't agree', a native English-speaker would temper this statement by adding, 'I'm afraid...' or 'I wouldn't go along with you there'. The Dutchman, although grammatically correct, thus tends to appear rude or boorish. This reinforces the sentiment that even a high degree of fluency is not necessarily the same as absolute bilingualism and that this latter level is rarely achieved.

The Policies of the European Community

Ten years ago the European Community consisted of ten nations, speaking seven languages; the translation of each of these languages into all the others involved no less than 42 language pairs!. This meant that every full meeting called for 42 interpreters and every single document had to be translated into seven languages. The accession of Spain and Portugal in 1986 added just two countries and two languages but, in so doing, increased the number of language pairs to 72 — almost doubling the load!

As yet, the EC shows no signs of reducing the number of languages but is actively encouraging the learning of other tongues through its Lingua programme. This, however, does not yet cater for the likes of police officers and their needs will probably have to be met in other ways, such as distance learning packs, (with or without supplementary tutorials) and attachments to other forces for assimilation by the 'total immersion' method. For police officers, the problems of language are compounded by the wide differences in laws and legal systems since international law rarely applies to the individual and domestic laws have to be invoked in most cases.

The Experience of Multilingual Countries

It is pertinent for us to pause here for a moment to consider briefly the position in countries which have more than one official language, such as Canada, South Africa, and Switzerland, as well as Belgium. The manner in which this fact affects the police will be considered in more detail later and, for the moment, let us simply consider some comments on the Canadian experience.

The use of both official languages — French and English — has received a significant boost with the passing of the Official Languages Act in 1988 which affirms their equal status in all federal institutions. The Act provides for the appointment of a Federal Commissioner of Official Languages and one incumbent, d'Iberville Fortier (1989), made the point that most French-Canadian city dwellers do become bilingual once they achieve a certain level of education. He further declared that his objective was to ensure that the necessary training opportunities were provided for all those who wished to take them up and help '...bridge the gap between the solitudes'. But, he added, '...there is no reason why Canada should even aim at having a majority of bilingual people. It is just not a realistic proposition. Nevertheless, Kingscott (1991) found that most Canadians approve of bilinguality, especially the young, and enrolments for language classes have substantially increased recently, providing a significant barometer of opinion.

This, then, is a brief description of the language barrier which is presenting so many problems to Europeans in general. In the ensuing chapters we shall be looking at how this problem specifically affects the various police forces and what they are doing (or proposing to do) to resolve the difficulties experienced.

2   The Barrier to Effective Policing

The Police Forces of Europe

'The Civil Police is a social organisation, created and sustained by political processes to enforce dominant conceptions of public order'.

Skolnick's (1972) definition of policing, quoted above, supports Bittner's (1970) contention that the specific role of the police in the enforcement of laws and the maintenance of order is as specialists in coercion, with the ultimate capacity to use legitimate force. This applies to all occidental policing systems, although those in Europe have evolved over the centuries and, in general, are all now based on one of two distinct types; the royal or governmentally-imposed, national system as exemplified by that in France, and the local, parochial system such as that on which the British system is based.

Despite the sometimes profoundly fundamental differences, one cannot necessarily detect any connection between the levels of democracy obtaining in a particular country and the specific model of police organisation and control adopted. In fact, England is very much in the minority among democratic nations in the degree of self-governance and discretion it gives to its police. The reasons for giving the police in the United Kingdom such a wide degree of discretion are manifold. For a start, as Reiner (1985) points out, they do not have adequate resources to enforce fully all the diverse and numerous laws. English law, no matter how precisely worded, needs interpretation in concrete situations; full enforcement would violate the generally accepted criteria of justice and the need to adapt the universal demands of the law to the locale. Strict law enforcement must sometimes be sacrificed in the interest of public tranquillity. However, it is clear that the extent to which a government directs its police can critically affect the style and nature of the force.

In the middle of the eighteenth century, most of Europe's absolutist rulers, seeking a model police force, looked to France. Paris appeared to be the best-policed city in Europe, using a highly-repressive system of *mouchards* or police spies. Given their entrenched notions of liberty which, they insisted, set them apart from most of the peoples of continental Europe, the English regarded the French system with horror; the last thing they wanted was something akin to the Paris Lieutenant of Police's spies or the *maréchaussée*, those militarised, mounted forerunners of the Gendarmerie who patrolled the provinces. The English were consequently one of the last to establish a police force in the modern sense of the term and, when the Metropolitan Police was formed in 1829, it was ostentatiously an unarmed, civilian force, wearing a civilian-type 'uniform' of top hat and swallow-tailed coat.

The evolution the French, or continental system of policing meant that, even where there was a national, centrally-controlled system, most countries had more than one police force, usually disposed functionally, the various forces having competence throughout the country as a whole (Belgium, France, Spain, Portugal, Italy, Greece, Luxembourg, Netherlands). In the cases where the police have evolved from purely local origins (UK, Germany) the police forces often continue to be established on a geographical basis, each force having competence for all aspects of policing within a prescribed area and, until quite recently, with no authority to act beyond a circumscribed area outside their own constablewick. Ireland is unusual in that it has a single, national force while Denmark has a number of local forces, operationally independent but with central control exercised over appointments, training, promotion and equipment. However, both of these countries, and their police forces, are quite small. The functions and organisation of the various European police forces are examined in more depth in subsequent chapters, which also review the level of linguistic ability to be found in them and the training initiatives adopted.

The difficulties raised through having a diversity of police forces are exacerbated by the fact that, even within a single country, serious inter-force rivalries have developed over the years which a common language does nothing to alleviate. This disturbing fact has been amply pursued and illustrated by van Reenen (1989), who quotes examples from Germany (*Bundeskriminalamt* v. the *Länder* forces), France (Police v. *Gendarmerie*), Spain (*Guardia Civil* v. municipal forces), Belgium (Judicial Police v. *Gendarmerie*) and the Netherlands (Ministry of Justice v. Ministry of Internal Affairs.

The most significant aspect of the Single Market, in so far as the police are concerned, is the complete or virtual removal of all internal border controls to facilitate the free movement of EC nationals between member states. That these citizens will include a proportion of criminals and other undesirables is self-evident, although it is unlikely that the removal of frontier controls will cause an explosion in criminality, since criminals tend to ignore them anyway. On the contrary, some see the existence of borders, such as that between the Republic of Ireland and Ulster and in the Basque region of Spain, as being a 'strategic resource' to (in this case) terrorists. What they do represent, in fact, is a major obstacle to effective communication between police forces and joint policing ventures. There may be an increase in thefts of valuable motor vehicles and similar property in areas close to certain frontiers but, on the whole, there is a cultural, or national, aspect to criminality and it is an increase in certain types of international crime which must be anticipated.

Although the whole question of the Single Market has been addressed extensively (some might say *ad nauseam*) in articles and books, most of these have concentrated on the opportunities for trade between Member States. Where the language question has been addressed, this tends to refer almost exclusively to how it affects businessmen or teachers. There is a tendency to ignore that fact that there is a pressing need for others, including the various police forces of Europe, to be able to communicate intelligibly with each other and that this requirement will intensify in the years to come.

Little or no empirical research appears to have been undertaken into the obstacles to police cooperation and the dissemination of criminal intelligence represented by the existence of nine languages. This is not to say that those closely involved with policing matters are entirely oblivious to the difficulties. Subsequent chapters will look at the extent to which those close to the problem — professional police officers and their advisers — have anticipated these problems and the solutions they propose.

Adversarial v. Inquisitorial Legal Systems

Any accountable policing system must, *per se*, reflect the judicial and legal system under which it operates. Lustgarten (1986) asserts that accountability is the degree of control various political institutions have over the police; there are other 'masters' such as the recognised police authority, the people of the area and the officer's own conscience, while Tony Benn (1991) neatly summed up the meaning of the word 'accountability' as:

(1) what are your powers?
(2) from whence do they derive?
(3) in the interests of whom do you exercise them?
(4) to whom are you answerable?
(5) how can we get rid of you?.

But Lord Denning, in a famous judgement (R. v Metropolitan Police Commissioner, ex parte Blackburn, 1968, 2 QBD 118), stated categorically that,

so far as the police in England and Wales are concerned, they are accountable 'to the law alone'.

This is where the dichotomy arises: in the same way that there are two
distinct policing systems in Europe, so there are two discrete systems of
criminal law which can only add to the problems of police collaboration.

The two systems are known variously as the adversarial/inquisitorial
systems, the Roman Law/Common Law systems, the crime control/due
process models and other, more fanciful names. To illustrate the essential
differences between the two systems, it is asserted that the function of the
accusatorial (i.e. Anglo-Saxon) system is to determine the guilt or innocence
of the accused. Under this system:

(1) the rights of the individual are paramount and the accused need not
    answer any questions (although this 'right to silence' is being increas-
    ingly challenged outside the fora of the courts);
(2) the trial is conducted by the 'rules of the game' promoting a childish
    and inefficient medieval idea of 'trial by conflict';
(3) the innocent must be protected at all costs, resulting in a system where
    there is a great divergence between what the police actually know and
    what they can introduce as evidence;
(4) there is a spurious sense of drama which encourages counsel to strike
    postures and indulge in sarcasm, and inspires judges to show bias;
(5) both sides seek to win and are not too particular how they do this;
(6) questions which could provide a short cut are often disallowed;
(7) the rules of evidence are very strict (which may tempt the police to
    'bend the rules' where it seems to them to be appropriate).

On the other hand, it is claimed that the inquisitorial or 'Continental' system
seeks primarily to determine the truth, and under this:

(1) the determination of the facts is paramount;
(2) the routines are simple and uncomplicated;
(3) it is the accused who is on trial, not the evidence presented. In fact, the
    initial enquiry, conducted by designated police officers under the
    guidance and direction of the public prosecutor or examining magis-
    trate, is so thorough that there is a strong presumption of guilt once the
    accused comes before the court. It is this fact which has given rise to the
    myth that, on the continent, the accused is guilty until proved innocent;
(4) the role of the defence and prosecuting counsels is very low-key and it
    is the court, and not counsel, which calls expert witnesses;
(5) the whole process aims to establish the truth and prevarication or
    refusal to answer questions is seen as an indication of guilt;
(6) the accused cannot plead guilty (or not guilty) and his guilt or inno-
    cence have to be proven, whatever he might say.

These wide-ranging differences between the criminal justice systems pose additional obstacles to cross-border policing as, even on the continent of Europe, the systems vary from country to country, even though they follow the same principles. Indeed, several senior European police officers cite the lack of judicial harmonisation as the greatest single obstacle to police cooperation. This phenomenon is not confined to Europe; even in the United States the police are hampered by the jurisdictional problems that arise in a country with thousands of police forces and where a clear distinction is made between state and federal crimes.

The Need for Communication and Collaboration

When one considers the academic theorising and occasional wishful thinking described in the previous chapter, it is easy to forget that language is not primarily an abstract construct or an instrument for artistic self-expression. On the contrary, Weber (1990) describes it as being primarily an everyday instrument of communication between people with scant knowledge of, and even less interest in, language itself.

Despite this self-evident but frequently overlooked fact, it is clear that, in the past, most of the police forces in Europe tried to ignore the need to communicate with their colleagues in adjoining countries, using an understandable form of language. Often this phenomenon arose from a sense of superiority, since most police forces consider themselves to be more than just a cut above the rest and have an inordinate pride in their record, history and procedures, but the lack of a common language was undoubtedly an exacerbating factor. The existence of land borders eventually compelled some forces to have limited dealings with their counterparts, albeit grudgingly and frequently fraught with difficulty.

In Great Britain, the police have always been particularly insular and current research suggests that, apart from a few, isolated areas which are particularly affected, this attitude has changed but little in recent years. It may therefore come as something of a surprise to learn that a Cross Channel Intelligence Conference has been held every year since 1969, involving English, French, Belgian and Dutch police officers — nearly a quarter of a century's commitment to international collaboration!

But the main reason for the reluctance to internationalise police work has been the sovereignty of the Member States and their monopoly of coercive authority; even urgent security matters tend to be handled in secret or via informal channels.

The practical problems facing the police have certainly not disappeared with the introduction of the Single European Act; indeed, the need for comprehensible communications and for greater understanding between the various police forces in Europe can only increase. This contention is supported by the fact that, certainly in the United Kingdom, the present-day forces have largely the same shape and organisation as they had in the nineteenth century, the only (crucial) difference being the fact that the lines of communication have been greatly extended, making effective communication much more difficult. International crime has been a growth industry in recent years and it is often better organised than some multi-national companies. Frequently it is so sophisticated that it is no longer feasible for any one State to try to combat it alone. The essential characteristics of this evolution include the degree of organisation demonstrated by some criminal groups and the vastly greater mobility of the individual criminal. This is true of both serious crime and petty offences; of shoplifting and pick-pocketing as well as drug-trafficking and art thefts; of major international fraud as well as the bilking of shopkeepers and hotels.

It is therefore imperative that the police service as a whole adopts some form of internationalisation in order to counter this phenomenon. What does this entail? For van Reenen (1989), a senior Dutch police official, police internationalisation means the process of extending police systems across national borders. He distinguishes three distinct types of internationalisation:

(1) *Cooperation*: this covers the gathering and exchange of information, the mutual provision of assistance in the form of personnel and equipment and the coordination of joint activities;

(2) *Horizontal integration*: this exists where police officers are given authority to operate in other countries or where the government of a country has authority over the police in another country;

(3) *Vertical integration*: this is where a police organisation is created to operate within the European Community — a form of European FBI or 'Europol'. We shall be looking at these possibilities in more detail later.

Once one accepts the need for a measure of collaboration, one has to determine the level at which it should take place. In its contribution to the House of Commons Home Affairs Committee's report (1990), the Leicester University Centre for the Study of Public Order posited three inter-related and equally important levels of criminal justice which require pan-European cooperation:

(1) *Macro*. Constitutional and legal matters

(2) *Mezzo*. Police and judicial operational structures, practices and procedures

(3) *Micro*. The prevention and detection of specific offences and crime problems.

All the various EC Member States have recognised these difficulties and problems and, without prejudice to the domestic legislation enacted within each state or to existing international agreements (especially the formation and operation of Interpol), they have agreed that multilateral collaboration should be developed between their police and security services. In particular, the Home Affairs Committee report referred to above points out that the Member States are agreed on the need for the creation of '...direct liaison methods by telephone, radio, telex and other means of communication'. They have not, however, pronounced upon the languages(s) of communication and, once again, this vital aspect has been glossed over. Non-verbal means of communication, such as telex, present only limited problems since it will usually be possible to obtain a translation in a reasonable time, but what happens when a Dutch police officer wants to speak direct to a colleague in Spain on a drugs-related matter, or an Italian detective finds a need to communicate urgently with a member of the Garda Siochana in Ireland regarding a shipment of arms to the IRA?

The concept of international cooperation was pursued by Sir Peter Imbert in his 1989 Police Foundation lecture, reported by Canning (1990), in which he asserted:

> ...We do not have a central unit officially established to receive and process non-drug crime intelligence from abroad and there is, we must admit, little coordination between various national indices. There has been a lack of investment, or slowness, in developing an overall intelligence strategy and perhaps even a lack of understanding of the intelligence concept itself.

Any proposal for improving police collaboration, especially in the sensitive field of criminal intelligence, must involve close communication between the various law-enforcement agencies and between individual police officers who, as we have seen, may be native speakers of any one of nine languages. Canning (1990) has posited that the four main methods which individual, non-linguist police officers adopt when confronted with persons who do not speak their own language are:

(1) The employment of sign language and/or simple words (often spoken in a loud voice).
(2) The use of an unofficial interpreter (e.g. school teacher, group leader, relative/friend or other party).
(3) Recourse to another police officer who has a modicum of language skills, if one is available.
(4) Obtaining the services of an official force interpreter.

The first is of little help where non-visual means are involved, such as the telephone or radio, while the others all necessitate calling on the services of a third party — a solution which may not always be entirely practical and will almost certainly be time-consuming and result in considerable delay.

Being separated from the mainland of Europe, the police in Great Britain have had less need than most to communicate with their European colleagues but the Channel Tunnel is all set to change that. The Kent County Constabulary, faced with the unique problems arising from the completion of this, the first and only terrestrial link with continental Europe, has identified the language barrier, especially as it affects verbal communications during emergencies, as one of the more serious of these problems. The solutions this forward-thinking force is proposing are covered in detail later.

Within Leicester University's concept of macro, mezzo and micro classifications, the macro level is outside the scope of this book but, at the mezzo level, one can readily identify a number of problems, such as the prevention of illegal immigration, drug trafficking and organised crime, together with some harmonisation of laws and judicial procedures. Some authorities stress the need to prepare and implement joint policies, the effectiveness of which must subsequently be assessed; others underline the equally important fact that those involved in the senior management of any organisation will have different language learning needs from those of subordinate staff, who may have a more superficial or merely social contact with visitors. Sir Roger Birch (1989a), the Chief Constable of Sussex and erstwhile chairman of the International Affairs Advisory Committee of the Council of the Association of Chief Police Officers of England, Wales and Northern Ireland (ACPO) visualises an urgent need for senior police officers to be able to exchange professional points of view, away from the political dimension which is present in groups such as TREVI (of which more later). Birch (1990) is also a proponent of the foundation of a 'Police Council of Europe', which would enable police officers at senior practitioner and executive level to meet on a regular basis, perhaps on the 'neutral territory' of the Interpol headquarters in Lyons. There is equally a growing need for the other elements in the various criminal justice systems, such as judges, public prosecutors, legislators, etc., to make serious efforts to find common ground and to facilitate the international enforcement of at least certain, more serious crimes.

The 'micro' (or operational) level is the one which most concerns us here and can be further divided into three separate areas: (a) the investigation of crimes having an international dimension; (b) the control of internal and external borders and frontiers; and (c) everyday contact with foreign nationals by patrolling officers.

There is good evidence to support the contention that crime control is the most important motivation for the internationalisation of police work, and calls for far more intensive cooperation between European police forces within the Community. The House of Commons Home Affairs Committee (1990) has identified drugs, terrorism and fraud as being some of the principal areas in which international cooperation is a necessity, but the Committee did not exclude other crimes such as counterfeiting, theft of vehicles and other high value items (including plant and machinery, antiques and *objets d'art*), extortion, kidnapping, pornography, arms and money laundering.

But to talk about policing purely in terms of crime is to miss the point of what the job is all about. Crime plays, in fact, but a small role in police work and one must not overlook the significance of road traffic, major disasters, major international events and public order. The then Home Secretary, Kenneth Baker (1991), in a Police Foundation lecture, claimed that simply to record what amounts to 25% of police activity (i.e. crime) as if it was all that mattered, presents a grossly distorted picture of what the police actually do and what the public expects from them. The Operational Policing Review, carried out in 1986, had already established that the service role occupied a major part of police time, at least in the United Kingdom, despite the 'fire-brigade' style of policing introduced by Unit Beat Policing in the 1960s. The acceptance of this fact by the police in the United Kingdom has resulted in them referring to themselves as the police 'service' rather than the police force, and the introduction of various charters, statements of common purpose and values, and a statement of ethical principles, etc. One survey, carried out in Essex, revealed that between 50 and 73% of all calls on the police were service-oriented. Reiner (1985), in his seminal work on the politics of the police, propounds the view that the historical and sociological evidence should have made it clear that fighting crime is not, has never been and could not be the prime activity of the police. The service aspect of policing is a natural by-product of the 24 hour availability of the police and their possession of coercive powers. In Reiner's view, 'To say they are a crypto-social work agency is like saying that sociologists are professional coffee-drinkers, because they spend so much time doing this'.

Paradoxically, research carried out by the Police Foundation found that people afford a higher priority to the avenging role of the police than they do to its helping role; it revealed that the view of the public is that it is important that the police catch offenders and answer emergency calls promptly. The core mandate of policing is not, however, merely the prevention and detection of crime but the more diffuse one of order maintenance (usually referred to in the United Kingdom as 'Keeping the

King's/Queen's Peace') and this was the fundamental reason for the formation of probably all the police and gendarmerie forces in Europe.

Apart from the Channel Tunnel and the Ulster/Republic of Ireland border, which is subject to a special relationship, Great Britain has no terrestrial borders. Entry into the country is via air and sea ports and passage through these is largely controlled by local Special Branch officers. Unlike most European nations, Great Britain does not have a specific police body to control its ports and frontiers and it is perhaps typical of the ambivalent attitudes of British bureaucracy that the country relies on officers from a branch of the police created at the beginning of the century to combat Irish terrorism to ensure that no criminally or politically undesirable persons enter the country. This country is also unique in requiring these officers to work hand-in-glove with a non-police body established to check the credentials of prospective immigrants — the Immigration Service.

The policing of land borders is therefore a matter which has previously only concerned the police forces in continental Europe and this task can be quite complex. For example, Germany has borders with fellow signatories to the Schengen accord (France, Benelux), a non-Schengen EC nation (Denmark), non-EC Western European states (Austria, Switzerland) and former Eastern bloc countries (Czechoslovakia, Poland). France, too, has six terrestrial borders but, in this case, mostly with fellow EC countries (Belgium, Germany, Spain, Italy, Luxembourg), only the frontier with Switzerland linking it to a non-EC nation. It also, of course, encompasses the continental terminal of the Channel Tunnel, linking it with England.

In all countries, the ease with which EC nationals will ultimately be able to move between EC countries must result in there being increased contact with foreign nationals at all levels, in the guise of tourists, businessmen, truck drivers, students, etc. As a consequence of this, the 'bobby on the beat' and motor patrol officers will find they have an increasing need to communicate with foreign nationals (especially fellow Europeans) who have become the victims of crimes, who have committed motoring offences, who seek directions or who are inquiring after lost property. It is reasonable to assume that, more and more, the ordinary policeman or policewoman will have to find the means to cope with foreigners who have lost their property, lost their way or 'lost their marbles'. It is also evident that not all of these will have an adequate command of the officer's own language.

There is also the question of day-to-day telephone enquiries, telex messages, access to data banks, etc. This means that, in addition to operational police officers, civilian telephonists, receptionists and certain other administrative or secretarial staff will need at least a passive vocabulary to enable them to recognise short, general messages and make appropriate responses. Interpol long ago recognised the problem by adopting three working languages (French, Spanish and English) in which it exchanges all information relating to crime and other ancillary functions.

Meeting the Perceived Needs

It is clear, therefore, that the general consensus of opinion is that a pressing need exists for the police to be able to communicate with and understand each other on a multinational basis, especially on the level of the European Community. This need, long neglected, is no longer entirely dismissed by the forces concerned or, perhaps more significantly, by their respective governments and police authorities. A number of accords have been entered into or agreed in principal which tend to fall into three distinct categories: global (Interpol), multinational (TREVI, Schengen, Europol) and bilateral/informal day-to-day collaboration (European Liaison Officers, Channel Tunnel, Anglo-Irish agreement, etc.). It must also be appreciated that many police forces already have direct communication with their counterparts in neighbouring countries, often through local or personal contacts, which they perceive as the most efficient method of working. There are noticeable gaps in this system, however; for example, the movement of goods vehicles throughout Europe is not supported by any traffic intelligence network or formalised system of contacts.

Interpol

Despite widespread misconceptions about its role and functions, the International Criminal Police Organisation (Interpol), remains the best-known example of a formalised, international agreement, and is clear evidence that the need for international police cooperation was recognised as long ago as 1923. Interpol has no territorial jurisdiction of its own but merely receives and passes on important criminal intelligence to its members around the world.

In the past, Interpol has had more than its fair share of critics, but the complaints often relate to matters which are outside the control of the organisation, such as a tardy response by the police service to whom an enquiry is directed. But the fact remains that an organisation which lists 'terrorist states' such as Libya amongst its members must expect to be seen as exhibiting a certain lack of credibility. Moreover, its very size and scope makes it open to complaints of bureaucracy and cumbersomeness. In the past these criticisms have been coupled with complaints concerning a serious lack of technology but this aspect has been largely addressed since Interpol's move to Lyons and average response time is now two hours as against 14 days in 1989. Indeed, the combination of its Electronic Archive System (which records criminal files on optical disks) and the electronic Criminal Information System puts the organisation in the forefront of modern technology as far as processing police information is concerned.

TREVI

In 1975, with the perceived shortcomings of Interpol in mind, the appropriate ministers and officials from the twelve EC Member States created an informal, intergovernmental forum, known as TREVI, where they can discuss '...cooperation at a practical, operational level against terrorism, drugs trafficking and other serious crime and disorder problems...'. Whilst this initiative was hailed as a major step forward in the control of international crime, subsequent critics of TREVI have complained that it is unduly ambitious, lacks accountability, selects its senior officers arbitrarily, has a peripatetic secretariat, an absence of archives and a paucity of support services. It is not a forum for police practitioners and is regarded by many as just another talking shop for self-important politicians. Certainly its progress has been very slow, due largely to problems of sovereignty and, while there has been a great deal of agreement in principle, there has been a distinct lack of real progress. There is a tendency to touch upon too many problems at each meeting and reach a conclusion on none of these. H.J. Bartsch (1989), a distinguished member of the Council of Europe's Directorate of Legal Affairs has suggested that the main problem of Trevi is one of identity. He asks, 'Who are they? They say nothing, there is no parliamentary scrutiny or control over them, they tend to be secretive. What are they doing?'.

In the same way as the Schengen accord provides for a multi-national criminal intelligence system, the police representatives on the Trevi working groups have been examining whether there is a need for a common European Information System (EIS), whether the needs could be met by existing systems such as Interpol, what the user requirements are, to what use the information would be put, what the potential legal and data protection problems are, and how willing would the various police services be to act upon the information supplied by their partners. The representatives from the Schengen countries have been keen to have the Schengen Information System adopted (see below) but this is resisted by the other nations.

Schengen

On a more local level, in 1985 representatives from the Benelux countries, together with those from France and Germany, met at Schengen, a small town in the Duchy of Luxembourg, to sign an agreement for the abolition of border controls between signatory States — a complete open border policy such as has existed between the Benelux countries since 1964. Although the agreement placed great emphasis on economic matters, it provided for talks to be held in the longer term with a view to reaching agreement on (a) police cooperation, (b) international legal aid and extradition, and (c) the search for common crime prevention strategies. In the fullness of time the agreement was signed by Italy (1990) and Spain and Portugal (1991).

The most innovative of the provisions on police cooperation concerns cross-border operations which are divided into two basic categories: surveillance and hot pursuit. Unfortunately, the implementation problems have proved largely intractable and, where agreement is reached, it often fails to take into account *practical* policing problems. The sub-group dealing with narcotics matters has run into difficulties because of the widely-varying levels of tolerance of drugs possession (liberal in Holland, strict in Germany); the sub-group covering arms and ammunition has run foul of the resistance shown by the French to any form of control over shotguns and the Belgians' refusal to disclose any information concerning their extensive arms dealings. The sub-group considering frontier controls has met with better success, although there is a distinct lack of harmonisation between the various bi-lateral and multi-lateral agreements which currently exist between countries and the problem of visa issues has yet to be fully resolved. Similarly, agreement has been reached in principle on the question of asylum but the participants have been unable to agree on the criteria to be adopted.

The proposed Schengen Information System, too, has been well received in principle but its implementation has run into considerable technical difficulties, coupled with concerns as to the data protection safeguards. In any case, it will probably be eclipsed by the Europol computerised information system, discussed below.

Europol

The opening of frontiers to neighbouring police forces, together with all the other problems of an 'open' Europe so far as policing is concerned, has led S.R. Baker (1988) to suggest that certain criminal offences should be codified as 'Euro-crimes', applicable to all Member States. This proposal has been supplemented by one for the creation of a 'European FBI' or 'EUROPOL'. Originally floated by the German government, one of the first proponents of this notion in Great Britain was John Alderson (1989) who opined that it may become necessary to develop a police organisation of a federal nature to deal with very serious crimes. It has been suggested that a body of this kind could undertake a number of coordinating functions.

The concept received a measure of political support within the Community, the Belgians, Spanish and Portuguese viewing it as a long-term possibility while the French regarded it as attractive in theory but probably unnecessary. In this country, Tony Mullett, currently Director of the National Criminal Intelligence Service, favoured the concept but Sir Roger Birch (1989a), speaking as chairman of the Association of Chief Police Officers (ACPO) advisory committee on international affairs, considered the suggestion premature and maintained that, for some years beyond 1992, the citizens of Europe would be unwilling to accept police officers from another part of the Community making active enquiries within their local community. He suggested that the way forward should be through structured evolution rather than radical change.

After considering all these points of view, the House of Commons Home Affairs Committee (1990) recommended that:

> ...the Home Office commission research to examine in detail the advantages of a police force acting in certain limited fields, such as terrorism, drug trafficking or fraud, across the whole of Europe.

The Government (1991) felt, however, that a police force operating across the whole of Europe, however limited in its scope, would raise enormous problems of powers and accountability and was '...not persuaded of the need for detailed research into the idea at this stage'.

The concept has refused to die however and, in June 1991, Chancellor Kohl tabled ideas, which were generally well received, for the establishment of a European Criminal Investigation Office (EUROPOL). There remains considerable resistance to the concept on the part of British senior officers who made a counter-proposal for the creation of a non-operational European criminal intelligence network. This viewpoint is, perhaps not surprisingly, also held by Raymond Kendall (1992), the British head of Interpol, who seriously questions whether a federal police system could work, given the different languages, legal systems and levels of accountability.

In the event, the Maastricht Agreement included a proposal to set up a body to coordinate certain police functions in all 12 European Community countries. At the outset, at least, this will be no more than a vast computerised centre for the exchange of intelligence on the movement of drugs and other international crime and a project team began work in Strasbourg in September 1992 to prepare for the launch of the Europol anti-drugs intelligence unit in 1993.

But even this limited measure of pan-European collaboration is subject to a variety of vicissitudes. The main difficulty is the need for unanimity: if just one of the 12 parliaments rejects the plan or any part of it, the whole system falls down. The British parliament is unlikely to be a problem; it knows that public opinion in this country will fully support tougher action in the war against drug-trafficking, even if this means giving the police increased powers. But this is not necessarily the case elsewhere; Spain still has vivid memories of Franco, East Germany has had experience of Stalin and the countries of mainland Europe cannot forget the Nazi regime. They know, in a way which those in the United Kingdom cannot, what happens when the police become too powerful and suspect that these quite modest proposals could be the thin edge of a very sinister wedge.

Channel Tunnel

Up until very recently, the Irish border was the only terrestrial link between the UK and a foreign country. This all changed with the completion of the Channel Tunnel between England (Cheriton) and France (Sangatte); for the first time it became possible to travel between the UK and continental Europe other than by air or sea; for the first time British and French police can work and arrest travellers in each other's country. Agreement has been reached for French police officers working at the Kent end of the Tunnel to carry firearms (unlike their British counterparts), and for plain clothes officers, both English and French to patrol the trains. It is this novel philosophy which has prompted the commissioning of the 'PoliceSpeak' study, which will be reviewed in more detail later.

ACPO European Unit

Established in 1989, the main functions of the ACPO European Unit are to gather and disseminate information relating to the Single Market, and to analyse and identify possible ramifications for the police. It issues briefing notes on a wide variety of subjects of primary or peripheral police interest and acts as an early warning system for police forces. This unit is complementary to the Metropolitan Police European Liaison Section (ELS) which was formed in 1976 as a result of German terrorist activities in Europe. The ELS is staffed by Special Branch Officers with a liaison officer from the French police. Its advantage over Interpol is seen as its high level of security in this very sensitive area of police work.

European Liaison Officers

Lack of significant progress with the Europol project prompts one to look more closely at bilateral agreements between any two countries. The advantage of bilateral agreements is that they can be implemented relatively quickly where there are time constraints, but on the other hand, their lack of uniformity makes them confusing for the police forces operating them or making use of them. In fact, one disadvantage of a bilingual Europe, or one where all speak a common language, is the observed tendency for clandestine cross-border police operations to be mounted where two countries share the same language.

To overcome the obvious difficulties related to sovereignty, the House of Commons Home Affairs Committee urged all forces in England and Wales to appoint European Liaison Officers (ELOs) and noted that, by 1990, all had in fact done so, albeit with mere tacit support in a few cases. However, the role of the ELO remains somewhat unclear, despite the Committee's recommendation that meticulous attention be given to the selection of appropriate ELOs and that the Home Office recognise their status. Research carried out by Canning (1990) for the Devon & Cornwall Constabulary revealed that ELOs ranged in rank from Sergeant to Assistant Chief Constable, while some forces nominated both senior and junior officers. Although much has been achieved in this respect, it is evident that there are still considerable 'grey areas' and the position leaves much to be desired.

These liaison officers remain stationed within their own force area and are not to be confused with the overseas liaison officers from the drugs intelligence units who work in countries other than their own and are referred to below.

Drugs Liaison Officers

As mentioned above, the appointment of European Liaison Officers in the various police forces in the United Kingdom should not be confused with the existing arrangements whereby Drugs Liaison Officers are appointed to work in other countries. These act under the authority of their home country, but in accordance with the laws of the receiving country. Such has been the success of this scheme that the British government has been recommended to review the experience with a view to developing it to include specialists in terrorism, fraud, etc.

Enthusiasm for this concept must be tempered by the views expressed by the British National Central Bureau of Interpol which, while recognising the value of liaison officers, felt they were expensive to run and unlikely to be able to cope with more than a small fraction of the cases handled by Interpol. It was suggested that it made more logistical sense to post liaison officers to Interpol headquarters or, where a particularly high degree of contact occurred, to the National Central Interpol Bureau of the country concerned.

Although a new idea in Europe, the United States has for many years posted FBI agents to their overseas embassies and these are now being supplemented by agents from the US Drugs Enforcement Agency.

The Question of Language

It will not have escaped the reader's notice that, in all the foregoing initiatives and projects, very little mention is made of the question of language. The British are renowned for their inability to speak foreign languages, although it is suggested that this is a question of frame of mind rather than ability, and that one must look to the educational system in this country to find the reason for this allegedly poor performance.

Nevertheless, there does exist a significant language barrier with, it is claimed, the worst offenders being the British who prefer to shout at foreigners in English, rather than try to learn their language. We in this country are reluctant to recognise the simple truth that, as the Prince of Wales (1990) has stated, knowledge of a foreign language is not an end in itself, but an essential skill for '...anyone seeking to make their mark...at international level'. To an increasing extent, this lack of bilingualism will be recognised as being a severe handicap.

The European Businessman Readership Survey (1984) showed that, whereas all Dutch business men and women could converse in a foreign language, only 12% of their English counterparts could boast this ability. Other major European countries varied between 35% (Italy) and 50% (West Germany).

This widespread lack of ability having been noted by Interpol, it decided, in the interim, to set up a European Liaison Bureau at the Interpol General Secretariat in Lyons to assist in urgent or complex cases and to promote better cooperation generally. The intention is that the bureau should include officers covering all the main languages and countries in the region, thereby hopefully overcoming any language obstacles. An officer funded by the UK is already working in this Bureau.

Professional Linguists

Given their lack of linguistic skills, British police officers have to place heavy reliance on the comparatively few competent linguists available to them, be they other police officers or professional interpreters/translators.

Article 6 of the European Convention on Human Rights provides that everyone charged with a criminal offence has the right to be informed promptly, in a language which he understands, of the nature of the accusation against him, and should have the free assistance of interpreters if he cannot understand or speak the language used in court. He must also be brought before a judge promptly and, in the case of Brogan v. the United Kingdom, the European Court held that four days was too long (the Prevention of Terrorism Act actually provides for detention up to seven days!).

The law in England and Wales recognises that the provision of an interpreter is a matter which also arises at the earlier stages of the criminal justice process. The interviewing and treatment of suspects in police stations is governed by the Police and Criminal Evidence Act, 1984 (PACE) and the various Codes of Practice made thereunder. In the case in point, paragraph 14 of Code C provides that, if the interviewing officer cannot himself speak the language of the person being interviewed, a person who has difficulty in speaking English shall not be interviewed except in the presence of someone 'capable of acting as an interpreter' where the subject wishes an interpreter to be present.

Where an interpreter is required, the services of a suitably qualified police officer or a professional or semi-professional translator have to be sought. However, the competence and availability of the latter are increasingly being questioned: How often are they used? How cost effective are they? How competent are they in their particular language? And what training have they had (or should they have) in the requirements of the Police & Criminal Evidence Act? As Sheppard (1992) points out, as yet the United Kingdom has no national scheme to select, train and monitor interpreters and translators for the legal system, although a steering group was formed in 1990, under the direction and funding of the Nuffield Foundation, to promote the wider use of interpreters in multilingual Britain.

A police or court interpreter needs an understanding of the relevant legal systems to use correctly even such apparently simple words as 'caution', 'magistrate', 'jury', 'plea' and 'binding-over'. Irving & McKenzie (1989) point out that all the PACE provisions which involve communicating with the suspect (for example communicating his rights and the responses to requests made) involve making judgements as to whether the suspect understands what has been said to him. Similarly, the things which have to be said to the suspect have a legal significance as well as a literal meaning so that discretion over how some things are said are not as wide as a lay person might imagine. This is particularly true when talking about the right to bail, or access to a solicitor, or the significance of signing a statement. If interpreters are not legally aware and particularly aware of the provisions of PACE, they cannot know where they have a degree of latitude in translation and where they must translate exactly what is said. Nor can they properly interpret the nuances of a suspect's replies. Police responsibility is not delegated to the interpreter yet the interviewing and custody officers cannot know what an interpreter is saying, nor do they know whether the interpreter is aware of the import of what he or she is doing. Responsibility for communicating rights to the non-English speaking suspect must, of necessity, lie with the interpreter.

The same writers quote a striking example of how an interpreter's personal affairs can interfere with his/her objectivity. In a case which required an interpreter, one of the authors was told by the interpreter that she needed to leave within an hour to pick up her children from school. The interviewing officer was unaware of this fact. The interpreter was asked to explain the position regarding legal advice to the suspect and she duly reported that the suspect did not require legal advice. At the conclusion of the interview, the interpreter remarked, 'I thought we would be here all night if she got a solicitor'. No-one involved in this case apart from the interpreter knew the terms in which the availability of legal advice had been put to the suspect. Confidence in the behaviour of the interpreter rested on the training she had received, and no evidence of this was available to the officers in the case.

Even this true account pales into insignificance beside the anecdote concerning a Mexican held by an American policeman on suspicion of having robbed a bank. Since the robber spoke no English and the policeman no Spanish the latter called upon a passing Hispanic to interpret. The robber admitted the crime but refused to tell where he had hidden the booty. In exasperation, the policeman put his pistol to the robber's head, cocked it and said to the interpreter, 'Tell him he has five seconds to tell me where the loot is hidden or I pull the trigger'. In terror, the robber stammered in Spanish, 'Don't shoot! The money is in the well behind my house'. The interpreter turned to the policeman and said, 'He say you one big mouth! You no scare him! Go ahead and shoot!'.

Although it is presumed (and hoped!) that this tale is apocryphal, it does vividly illustrate the way in which a non-linguistic police officer is entirely in the hands of his or her interpreter.

Despite their shortcomings, there is clear evidence that, even given improved linguistic ability on the part of police officers, the demand for suitable, professionally qualified and competent linguists will continue to grow. Since interpreters are *de facto* responsible for the civil rights of non-English speakers in custody, arrangements need to be made for them to be properly trained and officially certificated to demonstrate that they have at least a minimal knowledge of the appropriate legislation and their role in implementing its provisions. Without such training and subsequent certification the rights of speakers of foreign languages will be severely and unfairly diminished.

The Home Office White Paper Crime, Justice and Protecting the Public enlarges the activity of interpreters into the field of non-custodial sentences. In paragraph 7.8 it states: 'There should be a programme of discussion and activity for each offender' and it refers to the need for regular meetings of '...a group of offenders following a course of planned and structured discussions examining the causes and consequences of offending by each member of the group, and how offending can be avoided in the future'. Although not strictly a police matter and despite the fact that the proposal is undoubtedly directed principally at those persons resident in Great Britain whose native language is one of the Asian tongues, the concept does illustrate the importance of using qualified and competent interpreters throughout the whole criminal justice system.

In addition to interpreting interviews with suspects and witnesses in criminal cases, there will also be a growing need to provide Euronationals with information in the form of leaflets, multilingual crime and accident reports, etc., all of which will need to be accurately translated into the appropriate language(s) by professionally competent translators.

Language Acquisition

If it is accepted that the foregoing represents a *prima facie* case for language skills in the police service itself, the next stage is to consider how these skills might be acquired or improved. It is widely recognised that there is a great deal of confusion about how this can best be done, how much can realistically be learned, whether other language services could solve the problem better, and where one might go to obtain impartial advice on the formulation of a language policy.

These doubts are aggravated by the fact that there are no reliable statistical data within the police service as to the number of occasions police officers encounter situations calling for the use of a foreign language, what these encounters are and how the language differences are overcome. How often are Euronationals involved in crime or accidents; how many seek directions or advice or need to report lost property? This situation is not unique to this country but other European police forces have greater experience of cross-border cooperation and, dare one say it, much greater ability in speaking and understanding other languages.

Details of the various training courses and similar initiatives will be covered more fully in a subsequent chapter and it will suffice here to consider briefly the role of aptitude and memory in second language acquisition, the existence of memory variables and modes of communication. One must also look at the question of aptitude (which may be defined as a person's capability with regard to certain tasks and skills) and it must be emphasised that one cannot always assume that a person with a high aptitude for a certain skill will perform better than someone with a lower aptitude, since the latter might quite simply work harder at the task. Aptitude is, in fact influenced by a number of factors, including attitude, motivation and memory. Some experts have looked at the variations which occur in second language speech according to the task or situation concerned and have examined the communicative strategies employed to compensate for gaps in ability, such as gestures, phrase books, use of a third language, etc. Finally, it has to be stressed that second language acquisition is a relatively new field in which research is far from complete.

A number of European forces encourage officers to develop their linguistic abilities, either by paying for them to attend courses or by paying an allowance to those who have reached a certain standard. Most forces also identify linguists on recruitment. In considering the possible language tuition options available, an assessment needs to be made whether across-the-board training for police officers is necessary and whether it would represent the best use of scarce resources, especially if the skills acquired are not regularly put to use. The question of language training was considered by the House of Commons Home Affairs Committee (1990) which noted that a number of senior officers considered that the existing opportunities for language training in the United Kingdom were adequate and it agreed that it would be inefficient and unnecessary to train all British police officers in foreign languages. It was further noted that some forces were concerned that the learning of European languages could be detrimental to the acquisition of the minority languages spoken in this country, especially Welsh.

Following this philosophy, and prompted by the impending opening of the Channel Tunnel, the Kent County Constabulary has been involved in the development of a new, intensive French course for those officers who will come into regular contact with the French, based on a course run for the armed forces. This is covered more fully in the next chapter.

These views and initiatives underline the fact that the learning of a language is not merely an academic exercise. The skills acquired must frequently be put to practical use if they are to be maintained, and one needs to appreciate cultural differences, such as the use of first names and familiar terms of address, as well as the language of a country. In the police service there is also a need to understand the organisation, competence, responsibilities and accountability of the forces in other countries. The obvious and most attractive alternative to a global training scheme is to adopt a targeted approach, identifying those officers who would most benefit from, and could sustain, such training.

One excellent method of reinforcing existing language skills is the use of attachments and secondments to other countries, widely employed, for example, by the police in France and Germany. Kent has embarked on a limited programme of this type but the cost has been described as prohibitive. Nevertheless, the concept is supported by the Police Federation (1992) which has declared its support for exchanges of personnel between countries.

The acquisition of foreign languages by police officers is not, and cannot be, the solution to all language problems and consideration must be given to the extent to which language training can be supplemented by other solutions, such as the hiring of bilingual staff or the employment of external interpreters and translators. These solutions should be evaluated against the problems of training police officers, some of which are described below, including some which have already been touched upon:

(1) The time and expense involved.
(2) Changing language needs.
(3) Sustaining the levels of competence.
(4) Varied abilities and motivation.

Mechanical Means of Communication

The more mechanically minded or computer literate reader might suggest that the police should be looking at mechanical or electronic solutions to their language problems. But these present a number of obvious constraints and difficulties. Machine translation is still in its infancy and applicable only to fairly closely defined vocabularies, although Reeves (1989) stresses the possibility of (and, indeed, the need for) developing techniques in certain areas, and points to the Community's ESPRIT II programme for joint university work.

Clutterbuck (1990) has referred to the need to use computers and expert systems in anti-terrorist police operations and communications and describes the use of these at length in his book. But he, too, ignores the question of language, presumably assuming that the sort of intelligence detail included on any data bank would be intelligible without knowledge of other languages — an assumption which does not always stand up to scrutiny.

A more pragmatic approach is made in the report on the Kent Police 'PoliceSpeak' project submitted by the team from Wolfson College, Cambridge (1989). This raises the possibility of using a Bilingual Text Messaging System, capable of handling real-time operational communications across the language barrier and a limited vocabulary for this purpose has been produced.

In the modern world, contact between police officers (in whatever language) will often involve the use of some mechanical or electronic means of communication and the House of Commons Home Affairs Committee (1990) has already made a strong recommendation that Member States should create direct links by telephone, radio, telex, etc. This necessity for improved communications systems and data networks between police forces in the Community has been endorsed by at least one EC Commissioner, as a corollary to any plans for a central information system linking external frontier posts. Similarly, the Police Federation supports the development of information exchange systems, together with access to vehicle registration and licensing computers within the EC, without prejudice to the existing arrangements for cooperation through Interpol, the National Drugs Intelligence Unit and Special Branch.

The ideal situation, as described to the House of Commons Home Affairs Committee (1990) by an unnamed Portuguese police commander, would be for a rural police officer to be able to communicate directly by satellite with a common information system in another country. But, as a British Transport Police representative pointed out, communication systems and the language of transmission would both have to be standardised, and the notion, although attractive, must be regarded as very remote.

Sir Roger Birch (1990) has drawn attention to the fact that, at present, there is little or no technological compatibility even amongst the various police forces within single countries such as the United Kingdom. He opines that the police in the UK should be working in a coordinated way to develop the framework for an information technology infrastructure which will prepare the police for the future. This problem of incompatible computer systems is aggravated by a further difficulty: the differences in data control laws and confidentiality. The question of data protection has been exercising the minds of the police in the various European countries for a number of years now. For example, there are very strict data protection restrictions in Germany while the Dutch have somewhat looser requirements and the Belgians none at all; the German Border Police (*Bundes-*

grenzschutz) has access to the Belgian stolen vehicle index but any access the Belgians to the German system would be unlawful under German data protection laws.

Even if the police are given access to a joint computer-based intelligence system, or to the national computers in each of the other countries, there will remain a language problem. While computers may have a common language of their own, the peripherals clearly do not. Ordinary computer messages, like telex and fax communications, will need translating at source or at destination if the same language is not spoken at both ends. It is this fact which is currently occupying the PoliceSpeak team from Wolfson College, Cambridge, referred to earlier, which is working on a bilingual French and English computer communications system, for use in connection with the Channel Tunnel. A limited machine translation system has been devised which can convert set phrases from English to French (and vice versa) in real time so that details of any incident or accident in the Tunnel will be instantly available to the police on both sides of the Channel. The computer terminals show, in the operator's own language, which of the three tunnels is involved, the direction of travel, type of train concerned, presence or absence of fire or other hazards, the number of casualties and details of their injuries, etc.

The Effect of 1992 on Policing Policies

Whilst the largely symbolic gesture of removing the obstacles to free movement within the Community will bring obvious psychological and practical advantages to the citizens of the twelve Member States, it must not be allowed to reduce public security or jeopardise public order. Understandably, therefore, police checks at internal frontiers can only be eliminated if countervailing measures are taken to prevent the free movement of criminals, drug traffickers and terrorists.

There is a school of thought which holds that the perceived dangers of a frontier-free Europe are overstated and draws attention to the position in the United States, where free movement between states has always existed, despite the wide variations in state laws and types of law enforcement. If the European Community is a union of states without unity of government, it is equally lacking in unity of policing policies. And it is certain that, at present, there is no intention to impose a single language or otherwise ease the language problem.

The House of Commons Home Affairs Committee (1990) noted that the evidence it received was unanimous that free movement would have important consequences for the police. Nevertheless, it was noted that, in Spain, border checks had done little to apprehend and thus deter terrorists.

eland it was held that the land border was actually a strategic
:rorists and it was submitted that, unless policing policies are
as those which existed on the former East German border,
ire no deterrent to terrorists. On the contrary, it is evident that
iers often represent a barrier to communication and hamper
joint enterprises between the police forces on either side of them.

It is widely accepted that the major problems confronting the police have
been correctly identified as terrorism, organised crime, drugs, arms and
ammunition, coupled with a coherent exchange of criminal intelligence
between forces. One example quoted is the fact that a shotgun can be
purchased in a French hypermarket without any documentation or significant record made of the transaction and, presumably, then brought into the
United Kingdom without hindrance, despite the very much more stringent
regulations which apply in this country.

Both Belgium and France are opposed to any international exchange of
information concerning transactions between commercial arms dealer, no
doubt because of the importance of their national armaments industries.
Similarly, the different approaches to soft drugs to be found on either side
of the German/Netherlands border present a serious obstacle to rational
policing strategies.

Nevertheless, there is a manifest need for the police to be able to
exchange intelligence freely and speedily with their opposite numbers in
other EC countries in cases where a suspect is about to move across Europe
and where it is highly desirable that his or her activities and progress be
monitored.

These then are some of the problems which currently face the police
forces in Europe. And what of the future? Van Reenen stresses the need for
cooperation but emphasises that this must be implemented with sensitivity;
for instance, to use the German *Bereitschaftspolizei* to suppress riots in the
Netherlands would hardly be diplomatic in view of the painful memories
of their country's occupation which many Dutch citizens still hold. It is also
inevitable that attempts to encourage collaboration will result in a degree
of competition as to which system represents 'best practice', and will also
have serious implications for existing, national policing systems.

Another school of thought advocates a form of supranational police force
to deal with certain kinds of crime, while the more idealistic look to a future
in which there is one set of laws common to Europe, with freedom for the
police to operate without judicial restriction across the whole of a united
Europe in order to enforce them.

Considerable support has been expressed for a European Centre for
Police Studies which would help to identify and pinpoint those with special

skills or experience, such as multilingual police officers, and also to encourage the tuition of those who have demonstrated the capacity to learn a second language. Another question posited is whether the police should proceed towards internationalisation passively or actively, whether they should resist or support moves in this direction. Those who favour greater professionalisation of the police are convinced that active involvement is essential and that one will have to look across the borders — and even physically cross them — if one wishes to provide an effective policing service in the future. As an initial step towards this, ACPO supports the concept of a Police Council of Europe, which would enable police officers at senior practitioner and executive level to meet on a regular basis, perhaps at Interpol's Headquarters in Lyons.

The final word may be left to European Commissioner Sir Leon Brittan (1991) who concluded his Newsam Memorial Lecture at the Police Staff College in November 1991, by stating:

> The challenge for the British police is to turn their considerable talent, imagination and inventiveness to the question how best to increase the security of the UK without the familiar instrument of systematic controls at the internal frontiers. That effort...is forging new and valuable links with colleagues on the continent...(which) will enable Britain to meet its obligation to achieve full freedom of movement in the European Community.

Summary

It is clear, then, that there are already considerable problems facing the police forces of Europe. These problems will not disappear with the implementation of the Single European Act, the terms and effects of which have been well-rehearsed elsewhere. Indeed, the existing difficulties are more likely to increase and there will be a corresponding and growing need for quick and intelligible communication between the various police forces of Europe.

There are a number of almost insurmountable obstacles to an inter-force approach to the elimination of international and cross-border crime. These include the differences in organisational structures; differences in the goals, priorities and objectives; a lack of direct cooperation between forces coupled with the lack of a structured interface; a lack of coordination; poor means of communication; legal, political and financial constraints; lack of coherent leadership; sovereignty and national self-interest. There is also the fear, experienced by some outside the police service, that internationalisation could lead to excessive bureaucracy and a 'Big Brother' approach.

   This problem has been partially addressed by the proposal to create the
'Europol' data bank to assist with the coordination of certain police functions in the EC. This will eventually go some way to meeting proposals for
a standardised communications system, although how far it will meet the
demand for a standard language of transmission remains to be seen. The
view that the lack of bilingualism among British police officers will prove
a severe handicap is an argument to which we shall be returning later when
we look at the steps being taken to alleviate this problem throughout
Europe.

3 Great Britain

The Police System in the United Kingdom

Despite the existence of a few small constabularies established by particular statutes during the preceding decade (e.g. Oldham Police Act, 1826, Cheshire Police Act, 1829), the first significant English police force, in the modern sense of the term, is generally accepted to be the Metropolitan Police which was formed by Sir Robert Peel in 1829. A curious feature was the appointment of two joint Commissioners: one, a military man, Colonel Charles Rowan of the Light Brigade, and the other a barrister, Richard Mayne. These two idealists set high standards of entry and discipline which, to a greater or lesser extent, have been maintained over the years. The structure they created was based on a bureaucratic organisation (to promote professionalism) and demanded observance of the rule of law (implying the careful use of discretionary powers), the use of minimal force, an absence of partisanship (the police were disenfranchised until 1887), and emphasis on the service role. It also made provision for a measure of crime prevention through the 'scarecrow effect' which the mere presence of these 'New Police' provided.

Peel's deliberate policy of not recruiting men with the 'rank, habits or station of gentlemen' was designed to relieve the propertied classes of direct involvement in riot control (as members of the yeomanry or militia) at a time of intense class and political conflict. It also had the effect of incorporating the working class into British society (thus bringing an end to Disraeli's 'two nations'). It is not too fanciful to postulate that this policy, deliberately imposed or otherwise, still pertains to a certain extent in these modern times; a survey carried out by Cain (1973) established that the vast majority of recruits to the British police come from a working class background, albeit the skilled layer (few come from unskilled worker families while many are from white collar families).

Reiner (1982) quotes a survey carried out in 1980 which revealed that only a handful of the many graduate applicants were accepted and, consequently, only 4% of the police at that time could boast a university education. Around 10% had 'A' levels, 67% had some 'O' levels (or their equivalent) and just 19% had no formal qualification at all. The report of the Chief Constable of Kent for 1989 quoted the proportion of graduates in that force as 4.27%, indicating that there had been little change over the ensuing years. As will be seen from the next chapter, this compares adversely with the position which obtains in most other European countries.

Skolnick (1969) describes the average Anglo-Saxon police officer as an able, gregarious young man with social ideals, better than average physical prowess, having a rather conventional outlook on life, and with normal aspirations and self-interest. He is not a sadist or even unduly authoritarian. However, observers such as Colman & Gorman (1982) have noted that the police service tends to attract those with conservative or authoritarian personalities; the basic training has a temporarily liberalising effect but continued service results in the development of increasingly illiberal and intolerant attitudes.

The establishment of the Metropolitan Police in 1829 opened the door to the formation of a plethora of forces. By the latter half of the 19th century, every part of the United Kingdom was patrolled by either a borough/city police force or a county constabulary. Some of these forces were extremely small and it was not unusual for the whole force to comprise no more than three or four constables. Not surprisingly, such minuscule bodies were not very efficient and often included some not very prepossessing characters. Consequently, in 1889, most of the smaller borough forces were required to amalgamate with larger forces which, in practice, usually meant their being absorbed by the surrounding county constabulary. A further rash of amalgamations occurred during the Second World War, initially as an emergency measure, when many more small borough forces were compulsorily merged with larger neighbours. This process was pursued at various intervals during the ensuing years, notably following the 1974 local government reorganisation.

More recently there have been serious calls for a national police force, or at least a small number of regional forces. One widely-held view is that the police service has been structured into a number of ungainly conglomerates which embrace too many disparate, ill-defined and often incompatible functions. Will (1990) holds that national policing needs to be divorced from local policing matters and that it should be recognised that some tasks are so important that they should be handled from separate resource centres. The perceived advantages include the long-overdue modernisation of a creaking 19th century organisation, with a *de facto* rationalisation of the growing tendency towards central control over the police, plus an improved capacity for international collaboration,

So far this concept remains no more than an ideal for its proponents, although some see the introduction of the National Criminal Intelligence

Unit as the thin edge of the wedge. It is true, however, that the creation of an operational arm to this national body would be a radical departure from tradition — the effective formation of a national CID if not a national police force. Some very cogent arguments have been advanced in support of the concept of a national CID, with perhaps other policing duties remaining on a more local basis. It would certainly provide a useful platform on which to base future European police cooperation and would reduce the pressure to regionalise the existing police forces. The current Regional Crime Squads may be seen as a step in this direction, although the Association of Chief Police Officers (ACPO) is opposed to the idea of further amalgamation and the Home Secretary is understood to be of the opinion that the response to major crime can best be met by the Regional Crime Squads, with perhaps some detail refinements.

As for a national police force, covering all policing functions, the Home Secretary confirmed as recently as the middle of 1991 that he had no such plans and that such a move would entail an enormous administrative effort. But rumours of steps in this direction persist and cannot, at the time of writing, be entirely discounted.

As a result of these historical accidents, the United Kingdom is unique in Europe in having no national police force and more than 50 autonomous police forces with little or no national policy or control. The Home Office and ACPO issue certain, general guidelines but the chief officer of each force has a wide measure of discretion whether to adopt or reject such advice. The process of obtaining a coherent picture of what obtains in this country as regards the repercussions of the Single Market was much more complicated than that required for the rest of Europe. It was necessary to contact all the relevant police forces in the United Kingdom and so an approach was made to the Chief Constables of the 42 'regular' forces in England and Wales, plus the Royal Ulster Constabulary and three Scottish forces (Strathclyde, Lothian and Borders, and Dumfries and Galloway). As mentioned previously, the first two Scottish forces were included because of their size and importance whilst the views of the latter (very small) force were felt to be of interest, given that it had had significant, relevant experience in international liaison arising out of the Lockerbie air disaster. In addition, contact was made with the Chief Officers of the States of Jersey Police, the British Transport Police and the Dover Harbour Board Police, as well as the ACPO International Affairs Advisory Committee and the Home Office — a total of 50 involved bodies. All these were asked essentially the same four questions, as described below.

Of the 50 addressees, only two forces (Gloucestershire and Warwickshire) failed, despite reminders, to supply any response whatsoever —

sadly not even an acknowledgement. Of the remainder, six replied that they were unable to spare the time to respond to the enquiry but fairly comprehensive replies were received from, or on behalf of, the chief officers of the other 42 bodies (84% response) and these may thus be regarded as official policy or viewpoints. The responses may be summarised as follows:

Question 1: What do you see as the problems arising from the fact that the various police forces and judicial authorities in the EC speak different languages?

Not surprisingly, the responses to this question varied considerably, depending mainly (but not invariably) on the geographical location of the area for which the force was responsible.

Twelve forces (28%) felt there were no real problems as far as their force was concerned, usually because of the distance between their force area and the Continent, coupled with the lack of any air or sea ports within their area, while a few forces appeared to suggest that all Europeans speak English! Eleven forces (26%) considered that any problems which might exist could be ascribed to differences in legal systems and procedures, rather than to differences in languages, a point of view shared by a number of European police officers.

However, more than a quarter of the responding forces did foresee the need for effective communication, both verbal and data, while three stressed the need for a comprehensive understanding of European policing systems. Other forces made the point that much depended on the country involved (since there were few problems with countries like Holland or Germany where English is widely taught and spoken) and the level of interchange (the more senior European police officers often being able to express themselves adequately in English since they are usually better educated, given the common system of direct entry to senior rank for university graduates). One force supported the view that the greatest problems would occur at 'street level' where the lower police ranks had to deal effectively with foreigners without the aid of a readily-available interpreter. Only one force stressed the need to develop general language abilities, whilst another opined that the problems involving the ethnic minorities who are already in this country were of much greater significance than European liaison. (See Appendix 1.)

Question 2: Do you see these problems increasing once the EC internal borders have been effectively removed after 1/1/93?

A third of the forces considered that the removal of internal borders would have no noticeable effect. 10 forces (24%) saw any increase in problems as being a gradual evolution over time, whilst four others (10%) saw it as more a problem of volume rather than one of nature. Three forces anticipated a growing need to work closely with other European police forces whilst a similar number felt that any problems would be confined to those forces responsible for one or more major air or sea ports. One force saw the level of contact and interchange becoming increasingly lower, affecting more and more the 'man in the street'.An increase in cross-border operations was foreseen by three forces (7%) while another pointed to the likely rise in heavy goods traffic on the roads in this country, especially if EC plans to abolish cabotage arrangements come to fruition.

As might be expected, the Kent County Constabulary and the British Transport Police saw it as being more a question of the Channel Tunnel, rather than a consequence of the Single Market. (See Appendix 2.)

Question 3: Do you see accords such as the Schengen agreement adding to these problems?

Most forces appeared to see this question as relating specifically to the Schengen Agreement, despite the fact that it referred to a 'accords such as…'. Consequently, several forces were quick to point out that Great Britain is not a signatory to this particular agreement.

Some 25% of the responding forces did not see Schengen affecting the police in this country (or at least not their own force) whilst one suggested it had yet to be fully implemented in those countries which were parties to the agreement.

On the positive side, three forces felt the Schengen Information System would be a definite asset (although another three drew attention to the Data Protection problems which could arise). A similar number thought the accord would improve understanding and provide for the establishment of a system of 'best practices' on a European level, while another thought it would highlight the need for effective communication. Another force pointed to the danger of Britain lagging behind in the 'second eleven' of a two-tier Europe if it did not become a signatory. The ACPO spokesman suggested that the 'Europol' proposals could well eclipse the Schengen agreement and render it unnecessary.

With typical British reticence, three forces suggested that they would keep an eye on progress before committing themselves. (See Appendix 3.)

Question 4: In your force, what steps have been taken, are currently being taken or will be taken to alleviate these problems (e.g. language training, recruitment of linguists)

Given the diverging views on the Single Market expressed in the responses to the preceding questions, the reactions to this question were, not surprisingly, equally diverse and idiosyncratic.

Half the responding forces drew attention to the list of external interpreters which every force maintains. In practice, the type of individual figuring on such lists and called upon to interpret for the police varies from college lecturers or schoolteachers to the proprietor of the local Chinese 'take-away' or the foreign-born wife of a local Englishman with no linguistic qualifications or interpreting experience. As mentioned in the last chapter, this is a serious lacuna in the criminal justice system, as Irving and McKenzie (1989) have highlighted in their book on police interrogation. Although these listed interpreters are routinely vetted for their criminal or seditious propensities, seldom do they have any formal training, nor is their true ability professionally assessed.

It is encouraging to note that, in their responses, a few forces did question the competence of these 'interpreters' and the absence of any systematic appraisal or training. A few forces are particularly alive to this problem and are embarking on formal training programmes although, so far as linguistic ability is concerned, few police officers are qualified to make an expert judgement. For this aspect forces will probably need to seek professional guidance from one of the recognised, professional language organisations, such as the Institute of Translation & Interpreting or the Institute of Linguists. The longer term solution would seem to be the proposal mooted by Irving & McKenzie (1989) that police and court interpreters be formally tested and certificated, since the absence of such certification is likely to diminish the rights of non-English speaking suspects.

A recent development has been the emergence of a charity-based organisation operating under the name of Language Line. This body claims to be able to provide telephonic interpreting in a very wide variety of languages and no doubt could be of value in the initial stages of a police enquiry. However, the service (which appears to be mainly geared to medical matters and especially aimed at the Asian community in this country) would appear to have some very real limitations, such as the inherent difficulty in providing the face-to-face interpretation required for the taking of statements, the interviewing of suspects, etc. There is also the question of competence; it is claimed that the organisation uses 'fully-trained professionals' but it is not clear what is meant by this. It is asserted that the police help with the training but no force mentioned this in their responses to my enquiries. Certain professional interpreters have already expressed concern about the scheme and it would seem to fly in the face of proposals for *properly* trained and qualified interpreters for the very complex requirements of the police and the courts.

One can readily see how an organisation of this type could be of use in a situation where a patrolling police officer is confronted with a non-English speaker who wishes to make a complaint or report an incident, possibly as a matter of some urgency, and where the police officer can use a telephone to access the Language Line switchboard. But it must be looked upon as a form of 'linguistic first aid' and must not be regarded as a radical solution to the whole language problem. A report in the Evening Standard that use of the service would cost the police in London a mere £30–£40,000 instead of the £1.5–£2 million currently spent on providing interpreters must therefore be taken with a substantial pinch of salt.

No British force admits to an active policy of recruiting linguists and many follow the official ACPO policy which is that no general language training should be given to police officers. However, a few forces (including the Metropolitan Police) did mention that, where certain postings demand a degree of linguistic ability, an effort would be made to appoint those with at least a basic knowledge of the language concerned, with additional tuition being provided as necessary. This attitude is also reflected in the established Home Office policy concerning the selection of Drug Liaison Officers to work abroad and the arrangements made for these to receive extensive language tuition in the host country.

Other forces designate certain 'key posts' and provide language training for the holders of these. As an example of this, the Norfolk Constabulary is providing tuition in Dutch for a handful of key post holders — an uncommon choice of language, dictated by the number of Dutch vehicles arriving at the county's ports.

A number of forces provide part-time courses (mainly in French) for officers deemed to have a need (often Traffic Patrols), whilst one force has an officer attending a full-time degree course in Spanish (although this is probably a question of choice of subject made by the officer concerned, rather than a matter of force policy). The South Yorkshire Police has taken the apparently unique initiative of organising French and German conversation groups where members of the force can practise and hone their skills in these tongues. As has already been mentioned, one problem associated with the learning of a foreign language is the need for continual practice in order to maintain levels of fluency and this sort of enterprise is very interesting and encouraging.

The usual response to language problems, however, appears to be to 'encourage' police officers and civilian staff to follow a public course of language instruction at a local college or adult education centre. Such encouragement usually involves the granting of time off to attend lessons where these clash with periods of duty, and possibly some assistance with the costs involved. A fairly typical example is the venture introduced in No. 2 Area of the Metropolitan Police. Here, some 60 police officers attend weekly, two-hour sessions over 20 weeks, under the guidance of tutors from the Barking College of Technology, learning subject-orientated French, German and Spanish. Although allowed time off to attend classes when on duty, the students have to pay 60% of the course fee themselves. Emphasis is placed on practical police situations, leaning heavily on role-play techniques. The European Liaison Officer for that Area somewhat idealistically prophesies a scenario in which every police officer will speak, or at least have a basic knowledge of, a second European language and where police officers may apply for posts anywhere in Europe. Given the current official policy and the low level of language teaching in British schools, there would seem to be very little chance of this being much more than a pipe-dream for a long time yet, at least so far as this country is concerned.

Six forces said they would be keeping the position under constant review, while the British Transport Police and the Kent County Constabulary have both commissioned a comprehensive audit of language requirements/capabilities.

For many years now, it has been a common practice for police forces to issue bilingual or multilingual phrase books to all or some of their officers, usually traffic patrols. There is no standard phrase book available and most forces arrange for one to be produced by a local educational institute, with varying degrees of success. There seems to have been little, if any, research conducted into the effectiveness and utility of these and all suffer from the problem that, even if an officer is able to enunciate a particular phrase correctly, he soon gets into difficulties when the person he is addressing responds in his own language. Perhaps the best solution in this sort of circumstance is a card, similar to the type used by the Royal Canadian Mounted Police and described later, on which a few useful phrases can be pointed out (with no attempt at pronouncing them), with a number of possible responses similarly provided to which the interviewee can point.

Other forces mentioned the ACPO four-language lexicon of legal words and phrases which provides a list of some 900 English terms with their suggested equivalents in French, German and Spanish. The layout confirms the impression that the lexicon is intended for the English reader who wishes to find the appropriate foreign terms, rather than the other way round. The English terms selected for inclusion disclose some curious omissions and inclusions. Does the average police officer really need to know the foreign terms used to describe a magistrate's robe, to be able to find the appropriate terms for 'to indict something as false', 'to judge one's own case', 'optional subject', 'papillary mark', 'petty speculator', 'piece of wax' and so on?. Considerable space is devoted to the component parts of a firearm but little or nothing on motor vehicles or road accidents. By the same token, no translations are given for such common terms as criminal damage, wheel clamp, shoplifting, cocaine, chief constable, barrister, PACE, insurance, siren, probation, dog section, public road, drug squad — to merely pluck a few, everyday English terms out of the air. This work does not seem to have been drawn up or even checked by suitably qualified linguists and so also contains several serious mistakes and inaccuracies. It also suffers from the usual drawback inherent in multilingual dictionaries in that only one translation of each word is given, whereas in practice there are often a number of quite disparate possibilities. Unfortunately, this well-intentioned effort must be regarded as an object lesson in the need to use expert linguists for this type of work. As it stands, it is regrettably seriously flawed and, on occasions, positively dangerous. The lexicon of French/English terms produced by the Kent PoliceSpeak team (of which more later) is undoubtedly a much better bet for the operational police officer while translators and interpreters will find Ingleton's (1992) comprehensive dictionary particularly helpful.

The Police Staff College, Bramshill has, for a number of years now, been organising 'Policing Europe' courses (conducted entirely in English) at the College and several forces have sent officers on these courses which are also attended by personnel from the police in other European countries. They thus provide a useful, pan-European exchange of views but they are in no way a substitute for some form of language tuition.

Other British police officers, who possess a reasonable level of competence in the appropriate language, have attended similar courses organised by the French *Police Nationale* and by the German *Führungsakademie*, both of which are conducted in the language of the country concerned.

The 'Front Line'

Because of their very close involvement with Europe, two forces merit special mention at this point: the Kent County Constabulary and the British Transport Police, both of whom are directly and significantly affected by the opening of the Channel Tunnel. Because of this the questions posed to the other forces were, in these two cases, discussed and amplified at personal interviews.

The British Transport Police (BTP)

As mentioned earlier, the BTP are more concerned with the ramifications of the Channel Tunnel, rather than '1992' *per se*, although the two are accepted as being inextricably linked. Although not responsible for policing trains in the Tunnel or for the terminals, offences committed on through trains while on British soil are a matter for the BTP. Crimes committed on international trains (such as the theft of personal property or freight) are normally investigated in the country where the crime is reported unless the actual *locus* of the crime is known for certain. As the police at both point of departure and destination need to have details for their records the BTP foresee a demand for a mutually comprehensible (multi-lingual) crime report or a suitable system of machine translation. Experiments with the latter have so far proved too costly, although interest is being shown in aspects of Kent's 'PoliceSpeak' project (see below). The concept of a multi-lingual crime report is still being considered, however, although it is recognised that it will not be easy to compile such a document since free text must be kept to the minimum and optimum use made of 'tick-boxes' or similar solutions.

Apart from this type of written communication, the BTP do not antici-pate any great call for direct contact with their counterparts on the continent of Europe. The need for languages is seen more as arising in the field of police/public communication, in which it is necessary to differentiate between initiated conversations and the response to these; between action and reaction as it were. It is anticipated that most problems will arise where a police officer has to initiate the dialogue, usually in a prohibitive or interrogative form ('You can't go there!/Who are you?/What are you doing?/Where is your ticket?'). Difficulties will arise where the person spoken to refuses to comply or respond, either because he simply does not understand or perhaps because he considers he is justified in doing what-ever it is the policeman is objecting to. On the reactive side, where it is the foreigner who initiates the conversation, the patrolling police officer will need to be trained to be able recognise key words (taxi, train, platform, baggage, etc.) in other languages or perhaps be issued with a properly-researched and professionally-prepared phrase book or *aide-memoire* cards.

No difficulty is expected to arise where the injured party speaks English or has a reasonable command of that language but significant problems and hazards might arise where this is not the case. For example, the French term *vol* (theft) could easily be confused with *viol* (rape) by a non-French speak-ing police officer, with possibly disastrous results!

Despite its very active awareness of the language problem, the BTP regards it as being low on the list of essential attributes possessed by a candidate for the force. Consequently, it has no policy of directly and deliberately recruiting linguists into the force although, where a recruit shows a degree of proficiency in this respect it will be taken into account when deciding on postings and he/she will normally be assigned to an area where these skills will be of use, such as Waterloo station.

It is fully recognised that any form of language training at the operational level must geared to a perceived need and be cost-effective. Since British Rail already has a five-level language course, the Police propose to use the first level of tuition without adaptation for its officers, possibly modifying the second level to cater for their particular needs. However, two officers with a good command of French have already attended the French Police course at Clermont Ferrand and it is planned to pursue this initiative in the future in suitable cases.

The BTP has no doubt that the main demand at present is for a knowledge of French, with perhaps some German, Spanish and Italian. Other languages are only rarely encountered. However, current requirements and the ability to meet such needs are assessed biennially by means of a language audit. It is stressed that what is needed is some form of intelligible communication, rather than 'languages' *per se*, and that it is important to determine the environment which is prompting the need for communication (report of crime, lost persons, lost property, illegal activities, trespass, rail travel, etc.). A study has revealed that the demand for intercourse in foreign languages reflects almost identically the conventional breakdown of policing activities, i.e. crime plays a very small part, the service role being paramount.

Kent County Constabulary

As the force policing the corner of England closest to the continent of Europe, it is not surprising that the Kent County Constabulary has long been in the vanguard of cross-Channel policing liaison. It nominated a Cross-Channel Liaison Officer a quarter of a century ago and has either hosted or participated in an annual Cross-Channel Conference since that time. As the House of Commons Home Affairs Committee (1991a) noted:

> So far as relationships with the French police are concerned, we are aware from our previous enquiry into Practical Police Cooperation in the European Community, that the Kent Police have been particularly active in establishing contacts.

The opening of the Channel Tunnel provided an even greater impetus, given that, under section 14 of the 1987 Channel Tunnel Act, the Chief Constable of Kent has responsibility for policing the Tunnel.

The Channel Tunnel is unlike normal land borders which are relatively easy to define with fixed crossing points. Since the frontier between France and England is located under the sea at a point where it is clearly impracticable to establish controls, it has been agreed that there will be juxtaposed controls. This concept is examined in more detail in the next chapter.

Several years ago, in anticipation of the opening of the Tunnel, Kent formed a joint uniform/plain clothes Special Branch unit with a view to paving the way for the new border control duties — an initiative which the House of Commons Home Affairs Committee (1991a) described as 'innovative'.

Referring back to the concept of three separate areas of concern within the 'micro' or operational level of policing, at the upper level senior Kent police officers have for some time been actively involved in negotiations with the French police and gendarmerie (usually through the medium of interpreters) at the Cross Channel Conference and on the various Channel Tunnel Working Groups.

For their part, operational officers, especially detectives, are increasingly becoming involved in overseas enquiries and, to assist these, in 1991 a special European Liaison Unit was set at Dover to supplant the Cross-Channel Liaison Officer post mentioned earlier. This unit, which is in daily contact with its counterparts across the Channel in France and Belgium, comprises a detective inspector, two detective sergeants and two detective constables, all of whom are fluent French speakers, while some also speak German and/or Spanish. Although at present located at the Special Branch suite in the port of Dover, the Unit will transfer to the Cheriton terminal of the Channel Tunnel in due course.

The Unit's task is to provide support for the coordination of all aspects of European liaison within the force, to ensure that all the force's resources are used to maximum effect. Its specific responsibilities include the reception and assessment of information, intelligence and documentation, emanating either from its European colleagues or from any British police force, and ensuring its speedy dissemination. It makes arrangements for criminal investigations to be carried out in Kent on behalf of European police forces and arranges for enquiries to be carried out by European police forces on behalf of the Kent force (via Interpol or direct). It also assists members of the Kent force who require information regarding foreign nationals and their vehicles.

In 1991/92, the Unit handled an average of 140 enquiries per month, of which about 35 were on behalf on British forces and 86 in response to requests from France. The remainder related to requests from other European countries, notably Belgium. These enquiries provide an extremely useful starting point for any police operations which have a European flavour.

The existence of units of this kind does not, however, resolve the sort of problems experienced by patrolling officers when they have to deal with foreign nationals who are the perpetrators or the victims of offences. In this type of situation nothing can replace the value of at least a basic knowledge of the other's tongue, and the lack of a second language (especially French) continues to be a significant obstacle to the provision of an efficient and effective police service to foreign visitors to the force area, despite the widespread and often profound knowledge of English demonstrated by many educated foreigners. This problem is seen as likely to become increasingly acute in Kent following the opening of the Channel Tunnel.

Although the Kent force has no plans to target linguists in its recruiting programme, it is accepted that the possession of language skills would be a point in favour of an otherwise suitable candidate. Details of all personnel with such talents are entered on the force computer in either of two categories: (i) force interpreter and (ii) officers (of all ranks) with basic conversational skills. To qualify as a force interpreter, an applicant has to have passed the Home Civil Service language examination and successful candidates receive a language allowance. There is no standard test for those with 'basic conversational skills'.

Sadly, it does not seem that optimum use is made of these skills in determining postings although it has to be recognised that, when applicants were sought for two posts as Detective Sergeant Liaison Officers to work at the French terminal of the Channel Tunnel, a notice was published in Force Orders, written entirely in French!

Given the proximity to France, and the fact that French is one of the official languages of Kent's other close neighbour, Belgium, it is not surprising that the language most in demand is French (estimated to be around 90%) and this fortunately happens to be the language spoken by about half the qualified Force Interpreters (who number around 60 out of a force of just over 3,000 — or less than 2%), as well as the majority of the substantially higher number of officers (around 875 or 28%) registered as having basic conversational skills and who are able to 'get by' in a foreign language.

Over a period of four years, the force has provided courses in colloquial and vocational French for suitable 'key personnel' in a choice of two modes: (a) an eight-week residential (full-time) course providing 40 units of tuition, or (b) a part-time course over 40 weeks (also providing 40 units), both using professional language tutors from the local authority's further education service. Applicants for places on these courses are expected to be roughly of GCSE standard and are free to specify which mode interests them.

Entitled 'Salut les Flics!', the course was based on one used by the RAF at Cranwell but was specially designed for the force by experienced tutors from the Mid-Kent College of Higher and Further Education. It comprises a complete and comprehensive course book, a set of 40 audio tapes and a video tape. The latter was filmed largely in France, using real-life (unscripted) policing situations, mainly at the port of Calais. It is expected that, on completion of the course, the students will be able to:

• deal with normal social conditions in the French language
• socialise in French
• use and understand technical terminology related to police duties
• act as interpreter between English and French speakers
• understand written French.

The residential course was designed on a 'total immersion' basis, with an unused police house being placed at the disposal of the students in which everything is in French — notices, magazines, newspapers and all verbal instructions. It is gratifying to learn that, as a rule, the students enter fully into the spirit of things and continue to use the French language even in social situations, such as when drinking in the force club bar. One group even organised their own French 'Wine & Wisdom' evening in which a team of Assistant Chief Constables and other senior police and civilian staff took part (but failed to win!).

The extended French course followed the same curriculum but obviously lacked the total commitment and immersion of the residential version. In view of the fact that many of the students were from the Dover area, this mode was conducted at the South Kent College in Dover.

In all, some 150 police officers and civilian staff have received this form of intensive training and it is now considered that all the force's immediate needs have been fulfilled. The courses, which were expensive to run (about £10,000 per course) and made great demands on the students' time and effort, have been temporarily suspended. At some time in the future a survey will be made to determine future needs, especially once the Channel Tunnel gets fully operational. In the meantime, most of the former students are understood to be continuing their assimilation of the French language by voluntary attendance at night school.

A similar course, specially designed and organised for Operations Centre staff on a 30 week part-time day release basis proved to be less successful and experienced a high drop-out rate.

Other personnel, not regarded as 'key' personnel, are actively encouraged to pursue their own studies and the force has bought in a number of audio, self-study courses which may be borrowed by anyone interested. Additionally, members of the Special Branch (several of whom have attended the intensive course described above) visit the *Police de l'Air et des Frontières* in France in order to study and become acquainted with their methods and procedures.

Given the emphasis on European cooperation and the number of visitors to the area, it is somewhat disappointing that those officers who actually possess advanced language skills are not necessarily appointed to posts where they can practise, perfect or make effective use of this valuable talent. Under existing force policy as to 'tenure', it is understood that members of specialist units are not normally permitted to transfer to another specialist unit without an intervening period on ordinary patrol duties. Since these duties may well be performed in an area and/or in a post which does not call for the employment of language skills, it does seem that a valuable resource is being squandered in the very force where one would have thought it would have been most appreciated. The official view is that this policy will create 'a more omnicompetent workforce' but, as has been all too clearly demonstrated, few police officers in this country are, or ever will be, competent linguists.

Important as it is, mere knowledge of another language is not, in itself, the complete answer as Kent officers discovered to their chagrin at the time of the Zeebrugge ferry disaster. The official Kent County Constabulary report (unpublished) cites an instance of the difficulties caused through a lack of understanding of other policing systems and organisation:

> The first two Kent officers dispatched to Zeebrugge to fulfil a liaison role arrived at 0700 hrs on Saturday morning... Their instructions were brief: to present themselves to the Senior Officer in charge and offer whatever assistance Kent Police could provide. The officers had been dispatched on the assumption that the Belgian system, in broad terms,would mirror the United Kingdom system in terms of both casualty recording and of having a fundamental core of predetermined Police control and coordination. This basic expectation was not met and the reality of the system took time to understand.

The PoliceSpeak Project

No reference to the Kent County Constabulary would be complete without mentioning the PoliceSpeak project and, in order to do justice to this exciting initiative, it is dealt with in some depth in the next chapter. However, it is opportune at this point to quote the initial findings of the research team as set out in their report on Phase 1 of the project (Wolfson College, 1989):

> The most obvious communicative difficulty which can be foreseen when policing operations begin in the Channel Tunnel environment is the national language barrier. For the first time in history, the English-speaking authorities...will be required to work in physical proximity and constant daily collaboration with the French-speaking authorities

from France. Unless there is careful preparation, three particular factors may complicate bilingual communications:

(1) There is a limited number of bilingual people within the authorities charged with policing operations on either side of the Channel.

2) Of those officers who are bilingual in English and French, only some have experience of policing operations in both languages.

(3) The organisational structures and procedures of the two national authorities are different, as are the legal frameworks within which each works.

At first sight, the solutions to these complications appear to be:

(a) to increase the number of bilingual people within both national authorities;

(b) to provide experience for all bilingual officers in the policing operations conducted by the other nation's authorities;

(c) to familiarise officers within each national authority with the organisational and legal structures and operational procedures of their counterparts across the Channel.

The report goes on to analyse these possible solutions in more depth and suggest ways in which they might be implemented.

Conclusions

To summarise the general comments made by the various British Chief Officers (or their representatives):

(1) There is a need to train certain members of staff to be effective international liaison officers or investigators. This need tends to be concentrated on those areas which have, or are likely to have, close contact with the police or judicial authorities in other countries. ACPO sees the posting of detective officers to embassies abroad as a step forward in this respect.

(2) There is a need to improve language skills in the UK if the country is to influence European judicial policy and play a significant role in any kind of 'Europol'.

(3) There will possibly be a need in the future to consider the recruitment of EC nationals under the 'free movement of labour' provisions of the Single European Act.

(4) The lack of competent police linguists could mean that less serious crimes committed by foreigners will not be prosecuted in the future, due to the high cost of employing expert interpreters. Financial constraints could mean that professional interpreters will only be used for the more serious cases.

(5) The success or otherwise of the Kent PoliceSpeak project will be followed closely by many chief officers with a view to possible adoption by their forces, although it is recognised that the Kent force's requirements are probably unique.

(6) The value of exchanges and attachments to foreign police forces is acknowledged, although it is admitted that these can be frustrated by the 'politics of envy'. It is an unfortunate fact of life that, all too often, senior officers see visits abroad as a 'perk' rather than as a serious operational necessity or valid training requirement. It is essential that the officers responsible for arranging such visits ensure that the appropriate rank and linguistic levels are taken into account where exchanges or attachments are planned. If they are seen as merely a social jaunt, they will be doomed to failure and will lose all credibility.

Finally, it has to be stressed that the views and opinions quoted above represent the official policy. No attempt was made to interview officers of lower rank since few have any significant practical experience with this problem and their opinions are likely to be highly subjective and biased. Indeed, as we have seen, the need for European languages is not strongly felt in areas other than the extreme south-east of England, although the learning of other ethnic languages used in Great Britain may well be of close interest to police officers in areas with a strong Asian community, for example.

4 The PoliceSpeak Project

According to an unpublished report prepared by the team from Wolfson College, Cambridge (1989), with the collaboration of officers from the Kent County Constabulary, the aim of the PoliceSpeak project is to '...standardise and refine the language of police operations and so improve communicative efficiency and speed the flow of information with the ultimate objective of increasing inter-agency cooperation across national and linguistic frontiers'.

It is unfortunate that, as a result of inaccurate media publicity given to the project, a number of misconceptions have arisen about PoliceSpeak which need to be addressed. Firstly, it is not in itself a language; it is neither a mixture of English and French, nor is it an artificial language like Esperanto. It is simply a means of using natural language (initially English) more efficiently in a defined operational context. Secondly, it is not a closed system (like Air Traffic Control language) in which almost everything to be said is anticipated and prescribed. There has to be considerable flexibility in what may be said and prescription has had to be confined to a few essential items and general principles. Thirdly, although directly connected with and initiated because of the Channel Tunnel, it does not pretend to offer a total solution to all the communications problems which that great engineering project has raised, although it will considerably reduce the potential for misunderstanding and provide a more efficient use of the various means of communication employed in and in connection with the Tunnel.

History of the Project

The prospect of the opening of the Channel Tunnel means that, for the first time in recorded history, England has a non-maritime frontier with continental Europe and with a nation where English is not normally spoken. The communications problems resulting from this fact, together with the fact that an enormous number of people and vehicles are expected to pass through the Tunnel, was seen as ineluctably placing onerous demands on the Kent County Constabulary which, under the terms of section 14 of the Channel Tunnel Act, 1987, has statutory responsibility for policing the Tunnel. As a result, it was decided that a preliminary study of the likely communications needs of the force should be made, together with the possible means of providing these.

The study commenced in April 1989 and involved a combined team of Kent police officers and researchers from Wolfson College at Cambridge University. Funded by the Kent County Council and supported by generous donations from British Telecommunications plc, the team started by examining police operational communications records and assessing certain differences between the French and the English policing systems. The aim was to identify areas in existing communications practice which would have to be improved if communications in the bilingual environment of the Channel Tunnel were to be as efficient as they might be.

In the event, this meant analysing half a million words taken from actual operational communications in order to establish frequency of use and possible ambiguities. According to the team leader, Chief Inspector Roger Cruttenden, the initial feasibility study showed that, even in a monolingual environment such as the force radio network, there was considerable potential for misunderstanding. The study quickly discovered that there was no standard method of dispatching a police officer to an incident. Often the message from the Operations Centre was couched in terms such as, 'Can you attend, please', which could be interpreted variously as a question, a command or a request. The use of such terms in a multi-lingual situation would give rise to even greater possibilities of misunderstanding as can readily be appreciated when one remembers that *attendre* in French means 'to wait' and not 'to attend'

Having completed the feasibility study, the second phase of the project, started in May, 1992, aimed at producing, in addition to a report on the progress to date:

(1) A series of recommendations as to the practices and procedures to be used in Police radio and telephone communications, especially in connection with the Channel Tunnel.
(2) Providing the initial materials for the training of officers in these recommendations.
(3) An English–French lexicon of police terms, primarily designed for use in connection with the Channel Tunnel, but suitable for wider use as well.

The work undertaken in the second phase is described in more detail later in this chapter but, in brief, it comprised the following major aspects:

(1) Gathering data from a variety of police communications.
(2) Analysing the data according to a number of parameters.

(3) Investigating the Channel Tunnel as a communications and operational environment.
(4) Examining the differences between British and French policing organisation and practices.
(5) On the basis of the above, devising appropriate communications procedures.
(6) Preparing training materials.
(7) Training officers to use the procedures and evaluating their effectiveness.
(8) Making presentations about the project to a large number of different bodies and submitting half-yearly reports to the Consultative Committee.

The international dimension of the project was enhanced by the invaluable advice and assistance which the team received with the gathering and processing of data from the French, Belgian, German and Canadian police and from Interpol.

Although directly associated with the problems of policing the Channel Tunnel, it soon became evident that the work on PoliceSpeak had important ramifications beyond this limited sphere. The Kent County Constabulary therefore extended the project to include adapting the recommended radio procedures to the force's radio communications throughout other parts of the county. Other British forces have expressed an interest in the recommendations, recognising that PoliceSpeak has the potential to become a national, standardised form of communications procedure. And it is not only the police who are interested; other services with a responsibility for the safe running of the Tunnel are interested in the work and communications between the various emergency services are being, or have been, examined in the context of a major incident.

The other tangible result of the research has been the preparation of an English–French lexicon of operational police terms. The pre-publication version of this was very promising but needed extensive editing and revision, both as to content (restricted to what are seen as 'operational' police terms) and as to accuracy. It suffered from the lack of a French–English version but this has received attention and the final version should prove a useful and practical document. Whether it will be as useful to non-police interpreters and translators on both sides of the Channel as the compilers hope remains to be seen as it will have to compete with works such as Ingleton's (1992) dictionary. Nevertheless, the lexicon undoubtedly has the potential to become the prototype for other bilingual and multilingual lexicons for the police and emergency services, although here again, these will compete with such works as the so far unpublished French–German and German–French border police glossaries compiled by the staff at the joint French/German border control post at Strasbourg.

The Frontier

As we have seen, with the construction of the Channel Tunnel, Great Britain now has a shared terrestrial frontier with continental Europe. The Kent Special Branch has had a great deal of experience in operating controls at the county's existing points of entry and their basic role as regards terrorists and other such undesirables will continue in respect of the Tunnel. What will be different, however, is the way Special Branch operations are conducted. At Folkestone, Dover, Ramsgate, Sheerness, etc., persons entering the country are checked within the port area under British jurisdiction. Although the Kent County Constabulary works in close cooperation with its continental colleagues, the controls on either side of the Channel are independent of each other.

Up until now, all British ports have been separated from foreign destinations in both time and space. A passenger leaving Dover is checked by the British authorities before he leaves, boards a ferry and then passes into the 'limbo' of international waters before arriving at Calais where he is processed by the French authorities — in practice the *Police de l'Air et des Frontières* or PAF and the *Douane* or Customs service. A traveller by air undergoes a similar process with the controls at either end being separated by a flight through international air space.

Land frontiers do not conform to this model however and the Channel Tunnel will not even be of the usual type of terrestrial border. Most land frontiers are relatively easy to define with crossings being confined to clearly defined points where the border officials can exercise their controls within their own territory, independently of the neighbouring State. For example, as will be seen in later chapters, a crossing point on the Dutch–German border would have a German control point on one side of the border (a line painted across the road) just a few yards from the Dutch control points on the other side. In some places, such as the French–German border at Strasbourg, the two countries have set up a joint border control point, manned by officers from the police of both countries but, even in these cases, the border is clearly marked and the control point at or very close to this.

But the Anglo–French border is in the middle of the Channel and will be traversed at the mid-point of a submarine tunnel where it would obviously be impractical to set up even a joint crossing control point to process travellers. It has therefore been agreed that the answer must be juxtaposed controls. Although these do exist in a few other locations, their value as models is limited to a few practical arrangements.

The agreement between the United Kingdom and the Republic of France to construct a Tunnel is enshrined in the Treaty of Canterbury. This requires that '…the frontier controls shall be organised in a way which will reconcile, as far as possible, the rapid flow of traffic with the efficiency of the controls.' The requirement for a 'rapid flow of traffic' is paramount to the commercial success of the undertaking. The Tunnel will not merely be competing with the existing cross-Channel ferries but also with air travel and speed will be of the essence. For it to be competitive, delays caused by frontier controls must be kept to the minimum consistent with accepted levels of public security.

Towards the end of 1991, the British and French governments signed a Protocol with the formidable title of 'A Protocol between Great Britain and France Concerning Frontier Controls and Policing, Cooperation in Criminal Justice, Public Safety and Mutual Assistance Relating to the Channel Fixed Link'. This provided a framework for police collaboration in respect of the Tunnel, central to which is the concept of 'juxtaposed controls'.

Article 5 of the Protocol provides that 'In order to simplify and speed up the formalities… , the two Governments agree to establish juxtaposed controls in the terminal installations at Frethun…and Folkestone… These bureaux shall be so arranged that, for each direction of travel, the frontier controls shall be carried out in the terminal in the State of departure'. This means that, once a traveller has passed through the control at Folkestone, he will have unfettered entry into France, and vice versa, because both exit and entry checks will be carried out at the same place.

This represents an enormous change in the working practices of the authorities on both sides of the Channel. It will mean British police, customs and immigration officers travelling to France daily (there are no plans for them to reside in France). There, for 24 hours a day, 365 days a year, they will man the controls governing entry to Great Britain. Similarly, the French PAF officers and Customs officials will travel to Folkestone where, for the first time in history, they will carry out their checks on British soil and will be authorised to exercise their national powers of arrest, search and detention within the control zone. 'Breaches of the laws and regulations relating to frontier controls of the adjoining State which are detected in the control zone located in the host State shall be subject to the laws and regulations of the adjoining State, as if the breaches had occurred in the latter's own territory'. This means that, for example, a person passing through the control point in France who has in his possession a forged passport may be dealt with as if he were in England and even taken to that country to appear before the courts there.

Where an offence not connected with frontier control regulations is contravened (e.g. theft), the State having jurisdiction will be that in whose territory the offence occurred, including that part lying within the Tunnel.

This is why the British Transport Police have such a close interest in the whole Channel Tunnel project, as mentioned in the last chapter. The frontier lies at the featureless mid-point of a tunnel system approximately 40 metres under the seabed. Trains will pass through the system at high speed and, if an offence occurs on a train travelling through the Tunnel, it will, to say the least, be difficult to determine whether the crime was committed on British or French territory. It will therefore be impracticable to employ the test of 'location of the offence' as the sole criterion for determining jurisdiction and it will hinge on the 'point of discovery' or destination. The Protocol recognises this problem and, as a guide, suggests that when (a) it cannot be determined where an offence has been committed or (b) where an offence committed in the territory of one State is related to an offence committed in the territory of the other State or (c) where an offence has begun in or has been continued into its own territory, each State should have jurisdiction over the Tunnel and apply its own law. However, the State which first receives the person suspected of having committed such an offence (the 'receiving State') shall have priority in exercising jurisdiction.

Obviously, these arrangements will call for a considerable degree of liaison between forces and judicial authorities, coupled with an ability for each to understand what the other is talking about.

Major Incident Coordination Centre

At the Folkestone (Cheriton) terminal complex there will be a dedicated on-site Major Incident Coordination Centre (MICC) for use by the emergency services in the event of a major incident in the Tunnel. A similar centre will be set up at the French terminal (a *Poste de Commandement Opérationnel*). In the report of the House of Commons Home Affairs Committee (1991b) it was made clear that, in the event of an incident, the Eurotunnel staff would take initial control but would hand over to the emergency services as and when the latter arrived on the scene. In point of fact, so far as the British services are concerned, it is Home Office policy that the police should be responsible for coordinating the emergency services in any disaster or major incident which occurs anywhere in Great Britain.

Bilingual Text Messaging System

In giving evidence to the House of Commons Home Affairs Committee (1991b), the then Chief Constable of Kent, Paul Condon, referred to a number of scenarios which might be encountered in the Channel Tunnel context. A study of these, described in the Wolfson College report (1992) as a series of 'what ifs', has been submitted to the Home Office, primarily with respect to police powers. The study also contains, however, some important indications for communications, in particular identifying the points at which international contact between police officers is likely to be required. Almost all the 29 sets of circumstances make direct reference to Anglo–French liaison, in which the language barrier is seen as the most obvious difficulty. This will be particularly true in the event of a major incident which may well involve individuals who do not normally work in the tunnel and cannot be expected to have the language skills or know the appropriate terminology.

In view of this, one of the proposals covered by the PoliceSpeak Project is the introduction of what is described as a 'Bilingual Text Messaging' system in which a modest and dedicated machine translation system will be able to translate specially formatted messages into and from French. A small prototype was demonstrated in mid-1991 to illustrate the feasibility of such a system, recognising that the requirement for very clear and unambiguous bilingual communications in the event of a major incident in the Tunnel would benefit greatly from such a system. It also recognised that in the Channel Tunnel context a great many routine police communications will be effected between the British and French police, using both languages, and that these too could benefit from this type of system and the immediate translation which it provides.

It was therefore decided that a system capable of handling the day-to-day requirements and, where necessary, major incident situation reports, should be developed for introduction during the first year of the Channel Tunnel's opening. Such a development would not be possible were it not for the happy combination of technology and expertise available within the project team. PoliceSpeak is in the fortunate position of having access to a unique blend of knowledge and expertise in police communications and Channel Tunnel transport and communications systems, in rescue service procedures and in the linguistic demands of both countries, coupled with a significant knowledge of computer science and machine translation.

In practice, use of this Text Messaging System, with terminals at both ends of the Channel Tunnel, will enable operators to 'speak' to each other in real time without any knowledge of the other's language. This has obvious, exciting possibilities and, as the House of Commons Report (1991b) reveals, the other emergency services have already expressed an interest in the project since it is felt that it '…could considerably reduce the need for dialogue at senior level, being a reliable mechanical translation service which could be deployed to advantage by all the emergency services with but little adaptation'.

Here again, the success of this or any similar project depends entirely on the degree of cooperation afforded by the French authorities relying, as it does on the use of certain agreed and unambiguous words and phrases. Given the divergence between the languages involved and the widely-differing policing systems espoused by the two countries, the search for equivalence will not be an easy one.

The Bi-National Emergency Plan

During the construction phase it was found necessary to increase the contact with the French Authorities in order to devise an arrangement whereby, in the event of an incident in the Tunnel, emergency services from both sides of the Channel could work together. This resulted in the drawing up of a Bi-National Emergency Plan (BINEP). Based on an existing Kent County Generic plan which has been formulated between all the Kent emergency services in recent years, the Bi-National Plan reiterates the principles of the existing plans to ensure that responses to the Channel Tunnel are dealt with in exactly the same way as incidents above ground elsewhere in the county. The authorities were at pains to ensure that the operational procedures reflected normal arrangements as far as possible in order to ensure that personnel would behave as if the operations were taking place under United Kingdom standards alone.

Nevertheless, the Tunnel crosses a frontier and its policing involves another language and another culture. To facilitate communication in an emergency it is intended that the BINEP will represent the normal response to an incident in the Tunnel, being downgraded should the circumstances so warrant. So far as the British police are concerned, this means that incidents within the Tunnel involving the BINEP will be dealt with by officers communicating directly only with each other and other British colleagues, cross-language communication being handled by the Major Incident Coordination Centre (MICC). The Plan nominates a 'lead' and a 'support' nation, according to circumstances. In the event of an incident, the *Préfet* for the Pas de Calais *département* and the Chief Constable of Kent will consult with each other to determine which country will take the lead in resolving the situation, the other country acting in support.

Cross-Channel Liaison

As we saw in the last chapter, the concept of cross-Channel liaison is not new to Kent, but the Channel Tunnel project has added a further dimension and provided an unprecedented opportunity and means for the Kent police to further their cooperation with their colleagues in Europe. As a result, very close contacts at the highest level have been established between those responsible for law and order and emergencies on both sides of the Channel.

On an operational level, the situation is not so clear-cut. Few French police officers are really competent in English and, as we have seen, few British police officers, even in Kent, are adequately competent in French, although the training courses the Kent force has been conducting will go some way to addressing these problems created by the language barriers. There are at present no radio, electronic mail or other such direct links between the Special Branch Port Unit at Dover and their counterparts in France. Although the officers at the port are in daily contact with the PAF officers in Calais, most communication is by telephone, albeit some personal visits are made and some documents transmitted by facsimile machine. The PAF often ask for routine enquiries to be made in the United Kingdom, such as checks on the police National Computer (PNC) in respect of British vehicles found apparently abandoned in Calais, or for information concerning suspicious persons travelling between the two countries. Occasionally, more extensive enquiries are made in matters of joint interest which may involve Local Intelligence Officers in police forces elsewhere in Great Britain, other national agencies (e.g. National Drugs Intelligence Unit) or other bodies such as HM Customs and Excise. The Special Branch Port Unit is also asked by other British police forces to assist with certain enquiries involving persons travelling between the UK and France. An *ad hoc* liaison has been established with a peripatetic section of the PAF known as the *Brigade Frontière Mobile* which deals with enquiries concerning immigration and crime away from the passport control points. Criminal matters regarding the obtaining of evidence, taking statements, fingerprint searches, etc. are referred to the Constabulary's European Liaison Unit (see the previous chapter) or to Interpol.

No hard and fast rules have been established regarding the language of liaison. Where a French officer can speak good English he will use this language when telephoning to England and vice versa. Written communications such as fax messages tend to be in the language of the originator and are translated on receipt, which is probably a safer method than relying on an imperfect knowledge of the foreign language, with all the possibilities for error and misunderstanding which this can involve.

Basic Principles

Although the matters addressed in this chapter are concerned with different areas of police communication, they nevertheless obey the same basic, underlying principles, which include:

- Unnecessary variety of language should be avoided.
- Additional information should be provided to enable cross-checking (redundancy).

- Any possible confusion between analogous phrases used for different purposes should be avoided.
- The choice of a term should be made with the point of view of a non-native speaker of English being taken into consideration
- Existing good practices should be exploited and built on.
- Words or phrases should not be reduced by dropping syllables.

Avoiding unnecessary variety

The avoidance of unnecessary variety involves the introduction of a standard form of language to avoid any possibility of misunderstanding or misinterpretation. The recommendations regarding verbal communications recognised that three levels of language were currently in use: (a) officially prescribed language, (b) terms in common usage, and (c) slang, and these had to be taken into account when making any decision to impose a particular style of speech.

The research team found, for example that the word 'before' could be expressed as 'by the time (you leave)', 'by (six-thirty)', 'no later than (half-past)', 'prior to (the incident)'; 'once' and 'when' can both mean 'after' or 'as soon as' or even 'at the same time as' ('We'll sort it out *once* we get back'; 'Go in the back *when* I go in the front'). The phrase 'Let me know *when* he arrives' can be understood to mean 'Let me know *what time* he arrives' or '...*as soon* as he arrives', which is not the same thing at all.

Redundancy

By adding redundancy to a message unavoidably makes it longer to transmit and would seem to be contrary to the aim of providing speedy communication. However, if a message is misunderstood more air-time may be wasted in trying to get clarification. Sensible use of redundancy can result in overall saving.

Avoiding confusion

The choice of words or phrases is obviously influenced by the need to avoid confusion with similar terms which have a different meaning. One example is the distinction between calls to perform a particular action and the action itself. At present, the phrase 'Go ahead' is often used to mean 'Please continue with your transmission' but could be confused with an instruction to perform a particular action or go somewhere.

Position of non-English speakers

It will be noted that, although reference is made to the position of non-native speakers of English, this was not a fundamental imperative. The ultimate (and currently unresolved) aim of unambiguous equivalence of words and phrases in both languages calls for the full and unstinting cooperation of the French police in order to agree mutually understandable terms.

Existing good practice, etc.

The retention of good practices is self-evident, as is the desire to build on these. Similarly, it is important to ensure that words and phrases are not reduced as a result of sloppy speech.

Summary

In the event, what the PoliceSpeak project has done so far is to take steps to tidy up radio telephonic communication in English and, although previous attempts to impose strict radio discipline have all failed lamentably, initial reaction to these new recommendations appears to be favourable. In the course of trials conducted in selected parts of the county, the Kent County Constabulary (1992) reported that the use of the new system was proving its worth. Where the police had to evacuate some 80 people from a block of flats in Maidstone because of a security alert, use of the new system enabled the officers to deal with the matter much more quickly because there was no confusion over the radio. It is admitted, however, that, in practice, a number of modifications are being made to some terms. As one constable put it, 'It seems to be a matter of transferring the academic side of things into practice'.

Nevertheless, the PoliceSpeak Project represents a major step forward in terms of international police communications and will undoubtedly form the prototype for a number of similar schemes, both in Great Britain and overseas.

5 France and Germany

The other countries in the European Community have obviously had considerable experience in cross-border matters, something denied an island state such as Great Britain. The most important of the continental European countries are undoubtedly France and Germany, not only because of their size, both in geographical and demographical terms, but because they both have terrestrial borders with a number of other countries — an important factor in the present study. The questions asked of the various police forces in these two countries therefore differed somewhat from those asked the British forces and were couched in the following terms:

(1) What policing problems are currently created by the existence of land border with the neighbouring countries?
(2) Does the lack of a common language aggravate these?
(3) What difference will the removal of border controls after 1992 make to: (a) hot pursuit; (b) judicial enquiries.
(4) How many of their personnel speak at least one foreign language to at least 'A' level? What proportion speak which languages?
(5) Are the police personnel stationed on the borders required to speak the appropriate foreign language?
(6) What steps are taken to train personnel in foreign languages and will this change with the Single Market in prospect?

These questions were posed in French in the case of the two French forces and in English in the case of the divers German police forces. In the case of France this correspondence was supplemented or replaced by personal interviews in order to enlarge upon and clarify various aspects of the problem. Not all forces responded fully or specifically and the findings are set out below, country by country.

France

France is one of the largest countries in the European Community and, with six land frontiers, one of the more important for the purposes of this study. For this reason, and in view of its proximity to our shores and ease of access, much of the research was concentrated on this country and on its relations with its neighbours. The opportunity was taken to visit France on a number of occasions to research the subject in more depth and because I also wanted to determine whether police attitudes and procedures on the ground differed from the official policy as described in the correspondence I had received from the 'top brass' and related to me during my visits to certain administrative and training establishments in Paris.

Although many of the larger towns and cities employ a municipal police force, under the direct control of the mayor to enforce traffic regulations and local bye-laws, their powers and responsibilities are severely limited and, for all practical purposes, policing in France is entrusted to two national organisations, the *Police Nationale* with some 110,000 officers, and the *Gendarmerie Nationale* with perhaps 90,000.

The *Gendarmerie Nationale* is the direct descendant of the ancient *Maréchaussée* which patrolled the main roads of provincial, rural France in the seventeenth and eighteenth centuries. The modern force is divided into two main operational sections in addition to the largely ceremonial *Garde Républicaine* which is roughly the equivalent of the Household Brigade in England. The *Gendarmerie Départementale*, which is distributed throughout the country, is responsible for policing rural areas and the smaller towns and villages, as well as carrying out military police duties. Within its area of competence it carries out the full range of normal policing duties (crime investigation, public order, general law enforcement, traffic patrols, etc.). The *Gendarmerie Mobile*, like the CRS in the *Police Nationale*, provides a general reserve and is mainly concerned with public order duties and assists with the policing of major sporting, entertainment and similar events.

The *Police Nationale* now has four main operational branches in addition to the usual training, logistics and administrative branches. Of these, one (the CRS) is charged with public order duties and another (the DST) with State security and neither are therefore directly relevant to this study. The branch responsible for policing towns with more than 10,000 inhabitants, for port and border controls, and for the general intelligence service, is known as the *Police Territoriale*. Another branch, the *Police Judiciaire*, handles serious crime on a regional or national basis.

Since little information was forthcoming from the *Gendarmerie*, the data which follows are largely confined to the *Police Nationale* but this should not be seen as a serious constraint since it is the *Police Territoriale* branch of the latter force which is, as we have seen, responsible for border controls and for policing most border towns. As both are national forces the general policing policy, although handed down from different ministries (the Ministry of the Interior in the case of the police and the Ministry of Defence for the Gendarmerie), in fact reflects the same governmental strategies.

It is an important feature of the French policing system that, whilst it is a national one, members are given, in so far as is possible, the opportunity to serve in the area of their choice. Whilst some understandably plump for the luxury of the *Côte d'Azur* or, in the case of the *Gendarmerie*, some of the more prized overseas postings, the majority have a hankering to return to their native region. Consequently, members of the police and *Gendarmerie* serving in the border areas are often natives of that part of the country and so have a sound knowledge of the linguistic problems inherent to the region.

The problems which the existence of land borders pose to the French Police obviously vary according to the country concerned, the type of police service and the level at which collaboration is effected. At the very top, regular meetings are held with the directors of other European police forces but these are of a formal nature with professional interpreting facilities and thus few language problems are encountered.

At the operational level, the main problems are trans-frontier crime (especially drugs) and difficulties with tourists and other visitors. Where there is not a shared language, difficulties can and do arise and these are discussed more fully below.

For the sake of convenience, each of France's national frontiers with other countries is taken in turn (in a clockwise direction) in order to examine the specific problems which they pose.

Franco–Belgian border

Since the northern Belgian provinces are Flemish (Dutch) speaking and, since very few Frenchmen speak Dutch, it is freely admitted by the authorities that problems can and do arise here. The main point of contact for the French police is the *Gendarmerie Belge*, there being no equivalent of the *Police Nationale* in Belgium. Fortunately, since French is one of the other official Belgian languages, all Gendarmerie officers, and many of the other ranks are required to speak French and generally do so very well.

The main route between Paris and Antwerp (the A1 autoroute in France and the A14 autoroute in Belgium, jointly labelled the E17) crosses the border between Lille in France and Courtrai (Kortrijk) in Belgium. As such, this represents the principal link between these two countries and is on the direct route to the Netherlands and parts of northern Germany. For a number of years now, this very busy border crossing has been manned jointly by a section of the French *Police de l'Air et des Frontières* (known as the PAF and now part of the new *Police Territoriale*) and by members of the Belgian Gendarmerie. Working in adjoining offices, each with a full communications capability linked to the officer's own force, it is very evident to an unbiased observer that liaison and working arrangements are excellent. For obvious reasons, the working language is exclusively French.

In accordance with the declared policy of the French police, this border post is to be converted into a full *commissariat mixte* in the future, where the present somewhat *ad hoc* arrangements will receive official bi-national blessing, support and encouragement (including improved communications and increased financial support). Such has been the success of this experiment, that a similar shared station is being set up on the Valenciennes–Mons road, on the border with the francophone Belgian provinces.

The PAF in Lille have established exceptionally good working relations with the Belgian gendarmes across the border in Courtrai whom they visit on a regular, almost casual basis, sharing information and criminal intelligence. There is no evidence of any cross-border rivalry or petty jealousies. As mentioned above, because of the inability of the French to speak Dutch, and the excellent command of French which the Belgians possess, French is used exclusively as the language of communication — a good example of bilateral language arrangements. We shall be looking at this phenomenon again when we consider Belgium and the Belgian police in the next chapter.

The *Police Judiciaire* branch of the French Police is organised on a regional basis and is responsible for the investigation of all serious crimes committed in its area of competence. In the vicinity of the Belgian frontier much of this has a cross-border flavour and the *Service Régional de Police Judiciaire* for the north of France is able to benefit from these well-established contacts between the border control officers. Apart from criminal matters involving Belgian nationals, difficulties have arisen in the past where the Dutch are concerned. Although France has no direct border with the Netherlands, Lille lies on the direct route to that country and a great deal of illicit drugs traffic flows between the two countries. Since not many Dutch speak French and, as we have seen, few Frenchmen speak Dutch, problems of communication can arise. In such cases extensive use is made of the bilingual Belgian contacts who are often called upon to act as intermediaries between the French police and their Dutch counterparts.

For the general police personnel in large border towns such as Lille, the main problems include drug trafficking and the usual difficulties associated with tourists and cross-border shoppers. Since virtually none of these French police officers speak Dutch, English is frequently employed as a *lingua franca*. Once again, where necessary, the Belgian gendarmes at the

Lille/Courtrai border control point are called upon to assist, either with interpretation or with checks on a suspect's particulars and antecedents. Where other foreigners are involved, these are usually referred to the *Service Central d'Etrangers* (Central Aliens Unit) in Lille which, in addition to issuing aliens certificates and work permits, is responsible for all judicial matters involving aliens, such as illegal immigration or the use of forged documents. The unit includes fluent English, German and Polish speakers (in Northern France there are a good many descendants of the Polish miners who came to work in the area's coalfields in the early part of the century) and can readily call on Italian and Spanish-speaking police officers. Failing this, recourse is made to the list of sworn court interpreters, all of whom are language graduates, often teachers or lecturers. Where a recognised and permanently-sworn interpreter is not available for a particular language, *ad hoc* interpreters are sworn in for that particular case. These interpreters are the responsibility of the court and the police admit that neither type is tested or assessed as to their competence in the highly-specialised field of criminal justice work and, as in the UK, there appears to be no check on their actual, as opposed to mere paper, competence.

Paradoxically, the French police stationed on or near the Belgian border claim that they have more problems with the French-speaking Walloons from the Southern half of Belgian than with the Flemish-speakers in the North. Since the French regard the Belgians much as the English view the Irish, or Americans those of Polish descent, there may perhaps be more than a small element of prejudice in this!

Senior police officers in the border area have no regular contact with their Belgian counterparts. The Deputy Director of the *Police Territoriale* for the *département* (*Nord*) sees the ideal solution as being the formation of a central European Liaison Unit for France, on the lines of that established by the Kent County Constabulary at Dover, with which he was much impressed.

Franco–German border

Moving southwards, the industrial province of Lorraine has short borders with the francophone part of Belgium where there are no linguistic difficulties, and with Luxembourg which is equally problem-free. It has a much longer border with Germany, mainly Saarland but, although the local, German-based dialect is dying out, many *Lorrains* (as the inhabitants of this province are known) are fairly fluent in German, and so communication with the Germans over the border is not too difficult. The effect of this on police collaboration is dealt with in more detail later in this chapter, when we look at Germany.

Similarly, the local Germanic dialect is dying out in the adjoining province of Alsace, but many of the locals speak at least passable German. Since, as has been mentioned, a good proportion of the French police are stationed in their area of origin, many of those in Alsace and Lorraine share this expertise, although the Director of the *Police Territoriale* for the Bas-Rhin *département* (which includes Strasbourg), thought that perhaps only around 12% of his personnel could be described as German-speaking. What is more certain is that, as a general rule, Germans in the area do not speak French.

By far the largest town in the area is Strasbourg which is also the seat of many European and international organisations and bodies, including the European Parliament and the Council of Europe. It is also where the embryo Europol information system is being established. On the German side of the border is the Black Forest and, since there are no large towns or centres of habitation here, most of the tourist and criminal traffic is one-way, with a very heavy concentration on the city of Strasbourg. Consequently, most of the problems facing the police officers in the town are tourist-related. Major crime problems are passed to the local branch of the *Police Judiciaire*, whose greatest international problem is, again, the influx of drugs from Holland. Where the French police are in 'hot pursuit' of a suspect, the German authorities permit them to penetrate German territory for up to 10 km. Since, as has been mentioned, most crime is committed on French territory (i.e. in or around Strasbourg) the reverse seldom applies. On the whole, the authorities are not aware of any particular language problems, most matters being resolved by the knowledge of German possessed by the French police officers in the district.

Senior *Police Judiciaire* officers in the area hold high-level meetings with their German *Landeskriminalamt* counterparts at least twice a year and, given the relatively high number of Alsatians in the branch, linguistic problems are said to be minimal.

The main Rhine crossing between France and Germany at Strasbourg is the *Pont de l'Europe* or *Europabrücke*. At present there is still a small control point on the German side of the river but most work is concentrated on the French side where a full *commissariat mixte* has been set up, manned by both the French PAF and representatives of the German *Bundesgrenzschutz* (Federal Border Police).

The officers manning this crossing point are justifiably proud of the effectiveness of the cross-border collaboration with their German counterparts. They hold the view that, although exchanges of personnel and the forming of individual, personal contacts are helpful, the only real answer is units like theirs, permanently manned by officers with bilingual capability, which can provide a 24 hour service for contact with neighbouring forces. They make the point that, where one-to-one, personal contacts have been established, these are necessarily subject to absences on leave, sickness, etc. and cannot be 100% reliable, whereas a more impersonal, unitary system, can be reasonably sure of affording the necessary liaison, coupled with a high level of expertise. This reinforces the view expressed earlier that some form of bilingual or multilingual European Liaison Unit is the answer to most cross-border problems.

Since Switzerland is not yet a member of the European Community, it does not figure directly in this study but, as it is the German-speaking part of that country which borders on Alsace, the comments made above also apply here. The French-speaking cantons in the west of Switzerland have common borders with France and a long history of joint initiatives which obviates most policing problems between these countries.

Franco–Italian border

Although the border between France and Italy is quite long, it is mostly mountainous with only a few recognised crossing points. Most of the traffic passing between the two countries is concentrated on the Mediterranean coast route, between Menton and Ventimiglia.

Relations between the French police and the Italian *Carabinieri* are claimed to be generally good, although some French police officers actually working on the border expressed the belief that their Italian colleagues were not averse to ridding themselves of undesirables by directing them to places where they could cross into France unchecked.

On this border language is admitted to be a decided problem; few of the *Carabinieri* speak good French and, similarly, Italian is not widely spoken by French police officers. Where there is no bilingual officer on duty on either side of the border, enquiries and requests have to be resolved by *ad hoc* means such as sign language and the other non-verbal types of communication we discussed earlier. Liaison between the two police forces here is much less effective than that on the more northerly borders.

Franco–Spanish border

Much the same applies to the long, Pyrenean border with Spain. The two main border crossing points are near Perpignan to the south or between Biarritz and San Sebastian to the north, which helps to concentrate any frontier problems. According to the Spanish authorities, few of their police officers speak French (although it is in fact the most common foreign language spoken in Spain) but the handful that do tend to be found in the border region. Considerable reliance is placed on the ability of the French police to speak Spanish — something which, fortunately, a lot of them can do since many of them were born and bred in the area and are accustomed to communicating with their Iberian neighbours.

Language training

The official French view, as expressed by the Director-General of the *Police Nationale*, is that it is impossible to conceive any meaningful police cooperation in Europe if the linguistic barrier is not surmounted. The French police have therefore been taking significant steps to develop language training and have substantially increased the teaching of languages in its training centres.

Despite the existence of borders with several other European nations, as described above, English remains the language on which most effort is concentrated. Current training arrangements provide that all recruits to the national French police force receive a minimum of 40 hours tuition in English. In the case of trainee *commissaires* (superintendents), who are either direct graduate entrants or well-educated internal candidates who already hold fairly senior rank, they have a choice of English, German or Spanish. In view of their level of general education, these trainees often have a good knowledge of at least one foreign language already.

Where a recruit has no knowledge of English whatsoever, this basic tuition is increased to 80 hours. In the case of candidates for the PAF, although fluency in a foreign language (preferably English or German) is not demanded, it is seen as a definite advantage, provided all other requirements are met. At the end of the period of basic training, he/she undergoes a course of specialist instruction including, where necessary, a further 20 hours English tuition, specifically geared to the type of vocabulary encountered in their work and the type of person they are likely to have to deal with. This ranges from simple greetings and basic enquiries as to nationality, provenance and destination, to more complex, specific instructions ('Your dog must be kept on a lead'; 'It's a long way to Terminal 2: you'd better take the shuttle bus').

Where the duties of any other officer make it desirable, he/she may be sent for further language training on a full-time basis. Courses average 15 days and are mainly held at the Clermont Ferrand police training school where English, German, Italian and Arabic are offered, with Dutch being considered for the future. According to the Director of Personnel and Training for the *Police Nationale*, 51 improver courses in vocational foreign languages were held in 1991, attended by 530 officers, while 590 took the written and oral examinations (i.e. about 0.5% of the total strength of the force each year)

It is a regular practice to send suitable officers (usually of senior rank with a sound grasp of the appropriate language) on the courses held at the various national police colleges in England, Ireland, Germany and Spain. These are essentially professional courses, conducted entirely in the language of the host country. In addition, specific arrangements have been made at ministerial level for regular exchanges with the German police, incorporating both language training and familiarisation elements. Collaboration with Germany is particularly good and mutual bilingual liaison officers have been appointed, both at the various headquarters and on a local level.

Apart from these official, national initiatives, there are also various local language training facilities offered, usually on a voluntary basis, and geared to the needs of the area.

As will have been noticed, the emphasis is firmly on English and German, the latter being specifically aimed at those who are, or will be, working on or near the German border. Although a limited amount of instruction is given in Italian and even less in Spanish, in all other cases it is English which is taught on the grounds that this is the most useful lingua franca for general exchanges on the European level. English is, of course, the main language taught in French schools so many recruits have at least a basic grounding in this tongue which can be built on.

Germany

The Republic of Germany is made up of a number of *Länder* or largely autonomous provinces, six of which have common borders with other EC countries:

Schleswig-Holstein (Denmark)
Lower Saxony (Holland)
North Rhine-Westphalia (Holland and Belgium)
Rhineland-Palatinate (Belgium and France)
Saarland (France)
Baden-Württemberg (France)

Each *Land* is largely autonomous, with its own discrete police force(s) and legal system. There is additionally a Federal Criminal Police (*Bundeskriminalamt*) which investigates federal crimes such as certain currency offences, and a Federal Border Police (*Bundesgrenzschutz*), the latter being originally formed to patrol the borders with the former East Germany and other communist states but now undertaking more general border control duties.

Training for the members of the various *Länder* police forces is provided locally with the exception of the more senior ranks, for whom there is a Federal Staff College, the *Führungsakademie*.

In 1988 it was agreed that, as a matter of federal policy, all German police training courses should include tuition in English, French and the language of other neighbouring states where appropriate. The following year, the Ministers of the Interior for the relevant *Länder* agreed to ratify this federal policy and proceeded to formulate joint programmes for the exchange of police officers with their foreign neighbours.

The position appertaining in each of the *Länder* concerned is described below.

Schleswig-Holstein

Schleswig-Holstein is the northernmost state of the country, occupying the southern part of the Danish peninsular. As such, it is the only part of the European Community which has a common border with Denmark. The Schleswig-Holstein police claim that there are little or no policing problems with the Danes and the difference in language is largely resolved by the fact that the Danish police all speak either German or English, sometimes both.

Since Denmark is not so far a signatory to the Schengen Accord, there is no question of the police on either side of the border crossing it in the course of hot pursuit or for the purpose of surveillance or criminal investigations, except under the umbrella of normal, pre-arranged judicial agreements, such as formal 'letters of request'. Indeed, the fact that Denmark, as part of the Nordic Union, has an open border policy with the other Scandinavian countries (not yet members of the EC) is causing some headaches in the context of free travel within the Community. Swedes and Norwegians have a right to unfettered entry into Denmark and, if there are no controls on the Danish/German border, they will be able to pass freely into Germany and thence into all parts of the European Community.

As is the usual practice now in Germany, the Schleswig-Holstein police force normally recruits from those otherwise suitable candidates who have at least a sixth-form education and who therefore have already learned some English at school where it is a compulsory subject. During their basic training they receive a further 80 hours English tuition, concentrating on police and legal vocabulary. Those seeking promotion to the higher ranks receive a further 198 hours of English tuition and senior officers usually spend eight to twelve weeks in Great Britain as part of their advanced training.

As a result, the force is able to claim that pretty well all its officers speak English at least to a 'schoolboy' level, although it is admitted that very few speak Danish or any other language. There is no requirement for those who work on the Danish border to speak Danish since, as has already been noted (and will be addressed further in the next chapter), the Danes all speak English and/or German.

Lower Saxony

Lower Saxony (*Niedersachsen*) stretches from the North Sea coast southwards to the borders with the *Länder* of Hessen and North Rhine-Westphalia. The western side of the state borders on the northern part of the Netherlands, representing its only external frontier.

Nine out of ten applicants to join the Lower Saxony Police have been educated to the equivalent of 'A' level standard, with a compulsory pass in at least one foreign language. As a result all recruits have a solid grounding in foreign languages — mainly English. Where the exigencies of the service so demand, additional language training courses may be arranged and also many police officers take steps to improve their already significant language skills on their own initiative.

The border with the Netherlands presents few policing problems as there are good relations between the Dutch and German police forces. So far as language is concerned, many Dutch citizens (not just police officers or the population in the border areas) speak excellent German. However, this has not deterred the Lower Saxony force from arranging Dutch language courses for those of its officers who serve in the border regions.

North Rhine-Westphalia

North Rhine-Westphalia also has a common border with Holland and, further south, with Belgium. The police in the Land admit that these external borders do pose a number of policing problems which the effective removal of internal borders will do nothing to lessen. These post-1992 problems have been adequately rehearsed elsewhere and suffice it to say that the North Rhine-Westphalia police anticipate the same sort of problems (drugs and arms trafficking, organised crime, illegal immigration, road traffic problems, etc.) as the British and other European authorities.

The lack of a common language is recognised as an aggravating factor and, consequently, agreement was reached early in 1990, between the German and Dutch authorities for closer police collaboration. There are now regular exchanges and secondments, joint working groups have been formed and joint briefings are carried out. Intelligence is exchanged, joint contingency plans have been drawn up, direct channels of communication have been established and language courses arranged. The compilation of a specialist German/Dutch police dictionary is being actively considered.

Like their Dutch colleagues, most German police officers speak some English, which is a compulsory subject in most German schools. In addition, the North Rhine-Westphalia police organise special French and Dutch courses, which have proved very popular. Although a few officers already speak some Dutch, especially in the border regions, there is no formal requirement for personnel stationed on or near the borders to speak a foreign language. As a general rule, where joint operations are organised with the Dutch police to combat cross-border or international crime, they are conducted in German, or possibly English, rather than Dutch.

Although ratification of the Schengen Accord has been delayed through lack of agreement on points of detail, the Dutch authorities have agreed that the 'hot pursuit' of offenders may take place for a distance not exceeding 10 km inside the Dutch border where the alleged or suspected offence is one which is subject to extradition. The German police have a power of arrest within this area but only on a road or public place; they are not permitted to enter any private property for this purpose.

So far as the border with Belgium is concerned, this is comparatively short (about 50 km) and includes the small enclave of German-speaking Belgians in the area around the town of Eupen, the remainder of the Belgian border area being French-speaking. There are therefore few language problems on the Belgian border and collaboration with the Belgian *Gendarmerie* and Criminal Police is said to be very good.

Rhineland-Palatinate

This *Land* has a short border with Belgium (French-speaking part), and a rather longer one (around 120 km) with Luxembourg which, it is asserted, do not present any great policing problems. The chief of police accepts that a common language, used by *all* the EC nations, would be of benefit but the lack of this is not seen as a major problem. The removal of border controls is not expected to result in any great increase in either criminal enquiries or cases of hot pursuit, but it is nevertheless planned to increase the level of cooperation with neighbouring forces so as to minimise any problems and to avoid any security risks.

The authorities have no record of the number of officers who can speak a foreign language but it is assumed that most can speak at least one since all recruits need to have taken their school-leaving examination which includes a pass in one or more foreign languages. About 30% have received higher education (university or college) where a knowledge of at least two languages (one at advanced level) is required. The first foreign language in the overwhelming majority of schools is English, with French second.

In the Emergency Reserve section (*Bereitschaftspolizei*), this excellent grounding in foreign languages is enhanced by 44 hours of specialist training in English during the second year of their training. So far as the general police personnel (*Schutzpolizei*) are concerned, seminars in French and English are conducted at individual police stations. Given that the *Land* abuts Belgium and is also but a few kilometres from the French border, knowledge of French is regarded as vital and attendance at talks given by the French security forces are greatly encouraged.

To facilitate cooperation between the police in the two countries, the French and Rhineland-Palatinate governments signed an agreement in 1991 concerning 'language training and exchange of police officers for vocational purposes'. The aim of this agreement, which provides for annual exchanges for periods of up to three months, is to improve language skills and to give those involved an insight into the political, administrative, judicial and cultural structures of the host country, as well as into operational policing methods and practices.

Many of the officers serving in the border region were brought up there and have been familiar with the language of the neighbouring countries since childhood. To supplement this valuable core, and to increase the overall number of French-speaking personnel, some 100 officers attended basic or advanced French courses in 1991. Similarly, within the framework of the exchange programme, 10 members of the Rhineland-Palatinate force were attached to the French Gendarmerie for a three-week training period. In return, a similar number of Gendarmes were attached to the Rhineland-Palatinate police, initiatives which it is anticipated will be continued or extended in the future.

Saarland

Saarland is one of the smallest German states, with a population of just over a million, and lies adjacent to the French province of Lorraine. Since the 17th century the whole region has been continually fought over by France and Germany and it was not until as recently as 1954 that the people of Saarland voted to become part of West Germany, integration being completed in 1957. There are therefore very close links between Saarland and Lorraine which jointly formed this traditional battlefield.

About half of Saarland adjoins the Rhineland-Palatinate and the remaining half borders France (and a very small part of Luxembourg). The chief of police for the *Land* sees the main problem as the lack of a common legal system — not only where France is concerned, but with the other German

Land as well. The difficulties are compounded by the fact that some 9,000 foreigners commute from France into Saarland each day to work — more than twice the entire strength of the police force. In an effort to alleviate the problems, Saarland has joined up with Luxembourg and the Lorraine province of France to form a 'Saar-Lux-Lor' Euroregion and the frontier controls between these countries have for some time now been greatly relaxed, with only random checks being made. The complete removal of frontier controls should not, therefore, present any great difficulties.

Here, as elsewhere, the frontiers do not necessarily coincide with linguistic borders since it is reported that the Luxembourg police all speak German and, as has already been mentioned, so do many of the people in the border regions of the province of Lorraine. In some parts of Lorraine further from the border, however, the inhabitants speak no German and many of the younger generation no longer learn to speak the local Germanic dialect. It is claimed that many Saarland Germans in the border areas speak good French, but I have not been able to test this contention. Since the Saarland police authorities only claim 223 (6.5%) good French speakers in the whole force, this claim may be exaggerated and should be treated with caution. No doubt many do speak some French but whether this is of a standard to guarantee good communication skills is another matter. There is no doubt that, for historical reasons, the two languages are inextricably mixed in this long-disputed region but it would seem probable that, at least in the recent past, police liaison has depended to a very large extent on the ability of French officers in the area (many of whom are locals) to speak German.

Until very recently the Saarland police training programme was completely devoid of any tuition whatsoever in foreign languages, although direct entrants to the *Kommissar* (inspector) rank (who must have High School qualifications) are given 200 hours French tuition during their 2 year initial training. At the same time, serving officers who take the examination for promotion to *Kommissar* and who do not have a High School Certificate, receive 224 hours tuition in police-related French.

From 1994, however, French is also to be taught to the lower ranks in the course of their basic training. In the meantime, to cater for those already serving, 27 French courses and two English courses were run in 1990 and 1991, attended by some 350 personnel and it is intended that these should be continued for the foreseeable future.

Like their counterparts in certain other parts of Germany, the Saarland police have embarked upon an exchange programme with the French *Gendarmerie Nationale*. Under the terms of this programme, every other year, 20 *gendarmes* take part in a 14 day German language course and spend a further two weeks at a German police station near the border. In return, 20 police officers from Saarland visit the *Gendarmerie* during alternate years. There are plans to extend these visits in the future to include the *Police Nationale*.

At the same time, the Saarland *Bereitschaftspolizei* (emergency reserve police) have formed a 'partnership' with their counterparts in the French *Gendarmerie Mobile* squadron which is responsible for public order matters in the Verdun area. Similar arrangements exist with the Luxembourg police who are also going to serve part of their initial and further training with the Saarland *Bereitschaftspolizei*.

Baden-Württemberg

The *Land* of Baden-Württemberg has an extensive border with the Alsace province of France and relations between the French and German police have been highly cooperative for years. As long ago as 1977 the two countries signed a police collaboration agreement which includes the provision of mutual aid. Since 1990, the Baden-Württemberg government, together with those in Saarland and the Rhineland-Palatinate, has been holding discussions with the French authorities with a view to implementing the terms of the Schengen Accord. They have already agreed on or adopted a number of measures, including the provision of (initially) three shared police stations (*commissariats mixtes*) from which the police from both countries can offer a joint service. An example of this kind of initiative, at the *Pont de l'Europe* border control point over the Rhine at Strasbourg, has already been referred to.

Although the Baden-Württemberg police authorities agree that the lack of a common language is an impediment to effective police cooperation, they feel that the problem is much less acute than that which obtains on Germany's eastern borders with the former communist states of Poland and Czechoslovakia. Many police officers in the region have developed a working knowledge of French through having regular, private visits and contacts across the border and, as we have seen, German is extensively spoken in Alsace (which, at various times throughout its long and troubled history, has been deemed part of Germany). Using this core of linguistically-able officers, it is intended that French-speaking liaison officers should be on duty round the clock at certain German police stations, with a reciprocal arrangement across the border in France. This should obviate any problems arising from a lack of understanding although it does not go as far as a full *commissariat mixte*.

France's constitution prohibits foreign police officers from conducting criminal investigations in France and they will have to continue to use the formal 'letter of request' (*commission rogatoire*) system. The Schengen Information System will eventually help to alleviate this problem but, in the meantime, negotiations are continuing with a view to obtaining some relaxation of this rigid rule. The overall thrust of these is to intensify cross-border police contacts in order to enhance the exchange of intelligence and experience. A parallel anomaly arises in the case of hot pursuit since Germany allows the French police a power of arrest on German soil in such cases, but this prerogative is not reciprocal.

For the last 20 years, the Baden-Württemberg police force has recruited solely from those with a school-leaving certificate (equivalent of at least a sixth-form education), which has to include at least one foreign language. Prospective applicants who do not have this certificate can undergo a one-year, police-organised course in order to remedy this deficiency and so qualify for entry. All recruits therefore have at least a basic knowledge of English and/or French. Since 1990, the Emergency Reserve (*Bereitschafts-polizei*), has included further tuition in English or French (optional) during the second year of their training.

Thus it may confidently be asserted that virtually all the 23,500 police officers in the *Land* have at least a basic knowledge of a foreign language. About 8% have matriculated and, where candidates for promotion to the higher ranks do not have this standard of education, they attend a two-year in-service course to bring them up to this level. This course includes 260 hours tuition in the English language.

In 1990 voluntary French study groups were introduced but, as the main foreign language taught in schools is English, the emphasis tends to be on that language and around 80% of Baden-Württemberg police officers have at least a working knowledge of English while only 20% speak French. It is officially estimated that the proportion of officers who have a good or very good command of either language is around 14%.

It is obviously desirable that those serving close to the French border should have a command of French, but this is not mandatory. A rapid survey revealed that around 500 officers serving in the border areas had reasonably good language skills.

In addition to the tuition given to all recruits as part of their basic training, the following initiatives have been embarked upon:

(1) With a view to rectifying the anomaly whereby only a limited number of police officers speak the language of their immediate neighbours, the Baden-Württemberg authorities now provide a course of French language tuition at the police training school in Freiburg. It is considered vital that as many officers as possible, particularly those working in close proximity to the border, have a good command of French.

The course concentrates on police-orientated vocabulary and, in view of the lack of time available to provide *ab initio* courses, only those who already have a reasonable command of French (i.e. at least three years study at school or equivalent) are selected for official training.

Initially, participation is confined to certain key police divisions (Karlsruhe, Freiburg and the River police) in which between 400 and 500 police officers meet the required conditions and are interested in linguistic training. These have been divided into three groups according to priority, preference being given to those required to have contact with the French police in the course of their duties or who are likely to be nominated as liaison officers. These will usually be officers who are in charge of a station, a department or a squad, together with their deputies, plus members of the special intervention groups. The second group will be those more junior officers and civilian employees from the same areas who fulfil the required conditions as to language ability and, finally, the third group will be suitable officers and employees from the rest of the *Land*.

The course provides tuition over four separate weeks, each interspersed with four weeks normal duty, during which the trainees (not exceeding 15 on each course) are expected to consolidate the skills they have acquired. The course is conducted by a professional language teacher with assistance from other lecturers and an input from the French police. All candidates are tested by the teacher to determine the level of their competence before the course begins so as to provide a consistent level in each course. So far, over 100 police officers have attended this course.

Members of the special intervention groups with relevant French skills who are unable to attend the above course may attend the vocational French classes at the training school for middle-ranking officers at Göppingen. Where they lack the necessary knowledge, a special beginners' course will be held over one year with two hours tuition per week.

Other officers, especially those with no previous experience of French, are encouraged to enrol for courses at local adult education centres or similar institutions, with some financial assistance being given where the officer is likely to need the language in the course of his work.

(2) French is also offered as a core option (beginners and advanced) in the syllabus for senior officers at the Villingen-Schwenningen Police College. These students also have the opportunity of attending the six-week courses organised by the French Police at Clermont-Ferrand.

(3) A regular, annual exchange programme has been drawn up between the Baden-Württemberg police and the neighbouring legion of the French *Gendarmerie Nationale* as part of the Franco–German agreement for police language training and familiarisation attachments. Under the provisions of this agreement, in 1992 twelve members of the French Gendarmerie spent three weeks improving their vocational German at the Baden-Württemberg police training school, followed by three weeks practical instruction at local police stations in order to familiarise themselves with the organisation of the German police service and its practices and procedures. German officers selected for the reciprocal course in France are required to be good French speakers who are serving in a border area or on duties which bring them into contact with the French police. On completion of the exchange, all participants are required to report their findings and observations in order that the strengths and weaknesses of the programme might be continually assessed.

In view of the high priority which the Federal authorities in general, and the Baden-Württemberg Ministry of the Interior in particular, are giving to police cross-border co-operation, and the pivotal efforts made to overcome language barriers, it is not anticipated that these initiatives will be reduced in the foreseeable future.

Polizei-Führungsakademie

As mentioned earlier, the training of the more senior ranks in the various German police forces is carried out centrally at the *Führungsakademie*. Although not directly concerned in the policing of the country or with inter-force liaison, the *Führungsakademie* has an interest in the subject of languages in the police.

The *Führungsakademie*'s spokesman claims not to be aware of any general policing problems on the various German borders, apart from the matter of drugs from Holland. Nor was language seen as a difficulty as it is claimed that most officers in the border regions speak the language of the other country (although it will have been noted that this is not entirely borne out by the data obtained from the various *Länder*). Indeed, it suggested that the existence of local dialects (such as Alsatian) makes the bilateral form of communication the more desirable. The Academy does not anticipate that the Single Market or Schengen will make any great difference to the German police forces.

As described earlier, the German education system is such that most recruits speak at least one foreign language (usually English) to a reasonable level, and many speak a second tongue (usually French). A few speak

Danish, Dutch or even Turkish, Russian, Polish or Czech. As we have seen, this general grounding is built on at the police training schools and during an officer's service. The *Führungsakademie* confirms that officers serving in border areas are not normally required to speak the language of the neighbouring country but, in fact, many do. On the French border, the significant number of French natives who speak German (or a German-based patois) eases communication, while the Dutch are notoriously good at languages. Since German is a near-relative of their own tongue, few linguistic problems are experienced here.

Despite the fact that many police officers speak English, it is not considered that the imposition of this, or any other single, common language would be practical, except perhaps at major conferences. The existing and expanding bilateral and bilingual arrangements are seen as the best solution for the foreseeable future.

Conclusions

It is evident from the above that both France and Germany are well aware of the problems which the removal of frontier controls will present to the policing of these countries. It is also very clear that the police forces in these two countries are taking serious and fundamental steps to improve communication by a coherent programme of language training.

Germany has a certain advantage in that virtually all its officers have had the benefit of an educational system which provides a good grounding in a foreign language. The fact that this is usually English does not detract from the value of this education since it inculcates the regimen of language learning into the students, making the learning of another language that much easier. The German police therefore have the advantage of a sound knowledge of a useful *lingua franca*, plus a reasonable degree of competence in what is the most appropriate language for them, having regard to their geographical situation.

France has a somewhat less-advanced language learning ethic, although this is being rectified by the increased teaching of modern languages in the schools. Here again, the most usual language tends to be English, although students in border areas often have the advantage of learning Spanish or Italian where these countries are their near neighbours.

The French police has a three-tier system of recruitment, with candidates applying to join in the ranks of (i) uniform constable (*gardien*), (ii) uniform sub-inspector (*officier de Paix*) / detective sergeant (*inspecteur de police*) or (iii) assistant superintendent (*commissaire*). Qualifications for entry naturally vary according to the level, the lowest level merely demanding a school-leaving certificate. The middle tier requires a *baccalaureat* (multi-subject university entrance qualification) while candidates for direct entry to the third, or top, tier need to be graduates. In the *Gendarmerie* much the same applies with there being but two general levels of entry; commissioned and non-commissioned officer (all *gendarmes* hold military NCO rank).

As a result, the level of language competence in the French police and *gendarmerie* tends to depend on the rank; those in the lower echelons seldom having benefited from much language tuition at school, while the more senior levels will have had at least a basic grounding in a foreign language.

It is interesting to note that, in both France and Germany, all police officers are given at least some language tuition during their basic training with this being accentuated and increased in sensitive districts and in the case of key personnel. This compares with the official British policy of rejecting any language training at this level. Coupled with the parlous state of language teaching in most British schools, this results in most British officers having an almost complete lack of knowledge of any foreign language.

In the next chapter we shall be looking at the policing systems in the remaining European Community countries to see how these compare with their 'big brothers' in France and Germany.

6 The Rest of Europe

As we have already remarked, most European countries have had more than a little experience of cross-border crime and other policing problems and the situation in France and Germany has already been examined and compared with that which exists in Great Britain. There remain, for the purposes of this study, six other members of the European Community to be considered (it will be recalled that Greece, Ireland and Luxembourg have been excluded):

Denmark	Italy
The Netherlands	Spain
Belgium	Portugal

Contact was made with all the various police forces in these countries and the answers to similar questions to those posed to the French and German police were sought. It is perhaps worth repeating these here:

(1) What policing problems are currently created by the existence of land borders with (specified) neighbouring countries?
(2) Does the lack of a common language aggravate these?
(3) What difference will the removal of border controls after 1992 make to (a) hot pursuit and (b) judicial enquiries
(4) How many of your personnel speak at least one foreign language to at least A level? What proportion speak which languages?
(5) Are the police personnel stationed on the borders required to speak the appropriate foreign language?
(6) What steps are taken to train personnel in foreign languages and will this change with the advent of 1993?

The communications with Belgium, Italy and Spain were couched in the appropriate language while the others (to Portugal, Denmark and the Netherlands) were written in English. It is interesting to note that the use of the vernacular of the country concerned did not necessarily result in a better response. Denmark, the Belgian Gendarmerie and the three Dutch forces all replied very fully (in excellent English!). The results from the other three countries, despite the communication being in the appropriate language in two cases, were somewhat like the well-known 'curate's egg' —

good in parts! Not all the forces in these latter countries responded fully or specifically but what information has been gained is set out below, country by country.

Denmark

Denmark is in a unique position, being a member of the European Community and also part of the Nordic Union. Although staunchly European, it caused a furore in the middle of 1992 when the populace, by referendum, rejected the Maastricht Treaty. With a population of just over five million, it is one of the smaller Member States and has a common border with Germany (Schleswig-Holstein). Although there is a single, national police force, responsibility is shared between the national commissioner (*Rigspolitichefen*) on the one hand and the 54 district police chiefs (*politimestre*) on the other. These, and other senior ranks, are normally filled by external appointments, made from among members of the legal profession.

The Deputy National Commissioner maintains that there are no particular problems arising out of Denmark's border with Germany, nor does the lack of a common language give rise to difficulties. Denmark is not a signatory to the Schengen Accord and it is not clear at present how, and to what extent, the lifting of border controls in 1993 will affect policing. It is clear, however, that under existing law, only the Danish police have competence on Danish soil.

Denmark has a long tradition of language teaching, especially English and German, and the linguistic ability of recruits is quite good, some 40% having received schooling to an advanced level. These language skills are enhanced during the period of basic police training (which lasts over two years and encompasses both theory and practical experience). English is taught during the initial period of theoretical study and great importance is attached to the ability to use the language for the purpose of criminal investigations and for talks on policing and legal matters. Assimilation of this instruction is tested by examination. During the final, theoretical training phase, which follows a period of practical experience, further language lessons are given with the emphasis being placed on the sort of vocabulary likely to be required for police duties. Those who have already passed the English examination at a certain level receive this instruction in German.

To maintain and develop these language skills, the local police chiefs arrange further instruction in English, German and French (and other languages if deemed necessary) in collaboration with the local Police Language League, an association formed by the police organisations in conjunction with the National Commissioner. Officers whose jobs bring them into contact with foreign police and judicial authorities receive additional, advanced training, usually at the special language school run by the Danish Foreign Office. Senior officers regularly attend the language and familiarisation courses organised by the police colleges in England, Germany, France, Ireland and Spain.

Although no precise figures are available, it is clear that most Danish police officers are fluent in English and a large number also speak German. This means that, whilst there is no specific requirement for officers in the frontier region to speak German, they usually do so and there are normally no linguistic obstacles to police cooperation on the border. The existing, impressive language learning programme is likely to be maintained for the foreseeable future.

The Netherlands

One of the original members of the European Community, the Netherlands is steadfastly European and keen to cooperate with other Member States, a philosophy which extends to the police. It has common borders with both Belgium and Germany (Lower Saxony and North Rhine-Westphalia).

The language of the country, Dutch, is a low-German dialect which has been deliberately debased to a point where it is a distinct language. Any lingering connection with standard German was clinically amputated as recently as the 1940s, following the German occupation. Nevertheless, there is a good level of understanding between the two tongues, whilst the language usually referred to as Flemish spoken in Belgium is in fact a variant of Dutch.

So far as policing is concerned, there is one State police force, the *Rijkspolitie*, and a large number of municipal forces (*Gemeentepolitie*), although these are in the process of being amalgamated into a national force. There is also a military police force, the *Koninklijke Marechaussee*, which has certain responsibilities for border control, and a national Criminal Intelligence Service, the CRI (*Centrale Recherche Informatiedienst*) which is responsible, *inter alia*, for the collation of criminal records and intelligence, the coordination of major investigations, the maintenance of international police relations and for crime prevention advice. It also acts as the national central bureau of Interpol. Comprehensive and explicit responses were received from all three national forces, the municipal forces being ignored for the purposes of this study.

The Dutch police are very much alive to the threat from organised crime and a senior member of the CRI has warned that '...the growth of organised criminal activity in Western Europe can be regarded as the threat of the nineties'. This spokesman went on to say that he wanted to see the rapid development of cross-border crime-fighting, both through Interpol and through the EC's embryonic 'Europol'. 'It is my sincere wish that the international cooperation between law enforcement and criminal justice agencies develops at least at the same pace that it took our criminal opponents to internationalise their operations'.

In common with most of their colleagues throughout Europe, the Dutch see the differences in legislation and legal procedures which exist in the various countries as the most serious handicap to effective policing, given that the criminal is no respecter of national boundaries and, as mentioned above, is tending to internationalise his operations. These difficulties are partially offset by good police liaison, but they are far from resolved. Despite the legendary ability of the Dutch to speak foreign languages, the CRI sees the lack of a common language as significantly aggravating the problems facing the police in Europe, although the *Marechaussee* claims the lack of a common language does not significantly affect policing on the Dutch borders at present. This apparent paradox may possibly be explained by the fact that tourist and commercial traffic across Holland's borders seldom gives rise to any problems for the police and it is the criminal investigation sphere where a more profound knowledge of foreign languages is necessary to conduct investigations successfully.

The formal lifting of borders is not seen as being particularly significant since the Dutch police already have a large measure of freedom to cross the German and Belgian borders in hot pursuit. The Schengen agreement is seen as simply formalising existing arrangements. For the *Marechaussee* the main effect will be a significant reduction in their field of operations, responsibility for the southern and eastern borders being lost and all their efforts being concentrated on the nation's airports and seaports.

Although the *Rijkspolitie* claimed that 90% of its officers can speak one or more foreign languages, mostly German with English second and a smaller number speaking French, only the *Marechaussee* provided any rough estimates of the proportions speaking the various languages. This force claims that all its personnel can speak English, while about 60% speak German. Only 5% speak French. This tends to limit cooperation with France and, to a lesser extent, the francophone region of Belgium, although since the Belgian provinces which abut the Netherlands are all Flemish-speaking, this is of only limited consequence. As we have seen, it is not unusual for the Dutch and French police to use their Belgian colleagues as intermediaries, given the ability of the latter to speak both languages more or less fluently.

Despite this high level of linguistic competence, at high-level meetings, where matters of far-reaching importance are discussed, interpreters and translators are used to ensure there are no misunderstandings, although it is accepted that this does considerably increase the cost. On an operational level, the ability of Dutch police officers to speak English or German helps to reduce problems of communication.

Although there is no requirement for police officers serving on or near the German border to speak German, most in fact do so, as well as English. Given the high standards of language education in Dutch schools (English and Dutch are both compulsory subjects, with German and French available as additional options), there is little need for language tuition to be given to the police although the *Marechaussee* does support those of its members who wish to pursue a course of language study in their own time and pays half the cost of the course.

Belgium

One of the smaller countries in the European Community, Belgium has common borders with the Netherlands, Germany, France and Luxembourg. It also shares with Luxembourg the dubious distinction of having two major and one minor official languages — Dutch (Flemish), French and German, the latter spoken by the 67,000 inhabitants of a small area (some 854 square kilometres) near the German border. This latter group only became Belgians after the Great War through a border realignment.

This multiplicity of tongues has the effect of ensuring that linguistic squabbles are never far from the surface; for example, when the newly appointed Flemish-speaking minister of education wrote to his French-speaking colleague shortly after taking up office not long ago, he used the English language for his missive. This prompted a wave of self-righteous indignation, the Walloons accusing him of suggesting that no-one in the French administration understood Dutch while the Flemings upbraided him for making Dutch subservient to that international interloper, English. (In the event, the letter was a copy of a circular sent to all the minister's EC colleagues and, as they are all accustomed to speaking English whenever they meet, this seemed the most appropriate language.) However, this linguistic complexity does mean that Belgium is a useful microcosm of the difficulties which the police forces of Europe might expect to encounter in the future.

The policing system in Belgium is similar to that used by their Dutch colleagues to the North, the Belgians having a large number of municipal police forces of varying sizes, plus two national bodies, the *Gendarmerie Belge* and the Criminal Police Service. As with the Netherlands, the many municipal forces have been ignored for the purposes of the survey, but a very comprehensive response was received from the *Gendarmerie*. The senior official supplying this information (Major L Van der Stock, Deputy Director of Academic Studies at the Royal Military Academy) demonstrated comprehensively the excellent command of English held by officers at his level, although in his case this may be partly due to the fact that he had attended the Senior Command Course (essentially for potential British Chief Officers) at the Police Staff College at Bramshill.

Major Van der Stock stressed that, although he had been directed by the Commander-in-Chief of the *Gendarmerie*, the views expressed were his own and should not necessarily be seen as reflecting those of the General Command. Nevertheless, it was possible to confirm the accuracy of much of the data supplied during a brief visit to the barracks of the West Flanders group of the Belgian Gendarmerie at Courtrai (Kortrijk) in company with an officer of the French *Police de l'Air et des Frontières*. Here, the Captain in charge provided ample evidence of his command of French (his English was not put to the test) and one was able to bear witness to a practical demonstration of the excellent working relationships which exist between his force and his French colleagues.

One point of interest is the fact that Belgian law requires that police reports be written in the language of the region (Dutch, French or German) or, in the case of the Brussels, the language of the person concerned. Secondly, a person is free to use his or her own language when making a statement or laying a complaint, not just the three official ones, and every statement begins with the formula, 'I want to speak (language) and to use this language for judicial matters'. Where necessary, recourse is made to an official list, held at every police station and gendarmerie barracks, of translators who are competent and willing to be called in to act as a judicial interpreter. These are sworn by a police officer before every translation is made. But, in straightforward matters (e.g. traffic offences) the offender may simply be asked to write his own statement on the spot, in his own language. A series of leaflets in all the main European languages is available, explaining that an offence has been committed against the road traffic regulations, specifying the type of offence (excess speed, obstruction, failure to comply with a signal, lighting offence, breach of motorway regulations, etc.) and advising the offender that a fixed penalty is being imposed.

For internal gendarmerie communications both French and Flemish are used regularly for radio, fax and telex messages. Urgent transmissions are sent in the sender's language, followed in due course by an official translation, made by the national headquarters. All senior ranks have to speak both French and Flemish and also have a reasonable command of English and it is only at the lowest level that the possibility of a lack of comprehension arises, in which case it is claimed a multilingual colleague will usually be readily available.

The use of different languages in Belgium is so deep seated that there are seldom any significant practical problems with neighbouring states. In fact, the Belgian national borders are seldom contiguous with linguistic borders since the Flemish (Dutch speaking) region borders onto the Netherlands, the French-speaking region (Wallonia) has a common border with France, and the small German-speaking area borders onto Germany. Consequently there is frequently a common cross-border language. Elsewhere, such as where Flanders borders onto France, many Flemish-speaking Belgians also speak good French so there is seldom a lack of understanding. Indeed, the multilingual ability of the Belgians means that, where international coop-eration is called for at a high level, the Belgian police officers can usually speak the language of the other country or countries.

The Belgian Gendarmerie feels that the Schengen agreement might possibly affect relations through an increase in the sheer volume of work, much of which will need a degree of translation. It will become increasingly necessary to have recourse to the services of professional translators for the translation of foreign laws and court orders and this will become a signifi-cant item of expenditure and a drain on already severely limited resources. The need to hold more international conferences at the highest level will arise, calling for the use of simultaneous interpreters and the provision of suitable facilities for these — an expensive exercise.

As in Holland, the Belgian educational system places great store on modern languages. They are seen, not only as a vehicle of communication, but as a means of gaining a better understanding of other cultures and as a mental stimulus. With three different cultures within its national borders, this concept is regarded as indispensable to Belgium's entity and existence. It is not unreasonable to extrapolate this concept to the European Commu-nity.

The school-leaving age is the age of majority — 18 years, possibly the highest in the world. In the first year of secondary school, all pupils learn French or Dutch (whichever is not their native tongue), in the second year they learn English and many take German in the third year. However, it would be naive to assume that all Belgians speak two or three foreign languages; some students are simply not as gifted as others in this respect.

At present no language courses are provided for the lower ranks during their one-year basic training but this matter is being reviewed by the authorities, as is the possibility of paying a language allowance.

A direct entrant to the Gendarmerie at warrant officer level receives 100 hours tuition in the second national language, great use being made of language laboratories. Regular commissioned officers are required by law to speak both languages. It is assumed that the language used for their entrance examination is their mother tongue and they have to pass their qualifying written and oral examinations in the other language in order to be appointed second-lieutenant. During their five-year training period they are also expected to perfect their English.

Courses in these languages form part of the normal officer-cadet training syllabus and, as a result, every commissioned officer in the rank of Lieutenant, Captain or Commander has a good knowledge of at least two other languages. To advance to field rank (Major upwards) an advanced law examination must be passed in the officer's second language. For appointment to general officer ranks, and for some specific bilingual appointments, candidates have to demonstrate a 'profound knowledge' of both Dutch and French. This involves the passing of a very stiff oral and written examination, and the successful candidate receives a highly-coveted certificate known as a *professorate*. To assist suitable candidates, the Royal Military Academy has a special Language Centre while others may apply for time off to attend lessons and a refund of costs.

Language learning is not restricted to the official Belgian languages or to English. A few years ago a group of gendarmes took lessons in Arabic and even spent some months in Morocco to practise the language and study the culture. This initiative was prompted by the fact that there are a number of people of Moroccan origin in Belgium and the existence of some friction due to cultural differences.

Major Van der Stock's experience in attending the Senior Command Course at the British Police Staff College, although not common, is by no means unique. The Belgian police frequently send officers to colleges, academies and seminars abroad and, in the near future the Belgian Gendarmerie plans to send liaison officers to the main European capitals to act as an interface between the police forces in that country and their homeland.

It has to be appreciated that the practice of cross-border collaboration is not new to the Belgians; in fact it is nearly as old as the border itself. The Benelux agreement may be seen as the inspiration for the European Community and the Schengen accord is in fact merely an extension of existing Benelux treaties and agreements. The Schengen accord frequently permits the crossing of borders in the hot pursuit of offenders but only for a limited distance. In the case of Belgium this means that the pursuing police seldom find themselves in an area where a different language is spoken.

Italy

Italy is one of the southernmost members of the European Community and has the second-largest population, after the united Germany. It is a country which has been plagued by the presence of the Mafia and a history of corruption in high places. The Italian police has not escaped criticism, either, and Bayley (1975) claims that it is said that the Italian police are frequently associated with corruption, primitive measures and a lack of scruples; that they are feared and disliked and that one would hesitate to call on them except in an emergency. Whether or not this reputation is justified, the police in the countries which go to make up the European Community are being compelled to work in ever closer collaboration with each other and this will include the police in Italy.

Like most European countries, there is not just one but three main police forces in Italy: the *Polizia de Stato* (Public Security Guards), the *Carabinieri*, and the *Guardia di Finanza* (although the latter is mainly concerned with excise and customs matters).

The Public Security Guards date from the middle of the 19th century — an era when the nation itself was being formed out of a number of disparate states and kingdoms. It is mainly a uniformed force, although it does include some detectives who work in plain clothes, and totals around 80,000 personnel. It is divided into three main sections; the Territorial force, which is sub-divided into provincial groups to deal with normal policing duties; the Mobile Force, which provides a general emergency reserve and is particularly concerned with public order matters (cf. the CRS in France); and the Special Force which incorporates the Highways Police, the Railways Police and the Frontier Police.

The *Carabinieri* is even older than the Public Security Guards, being formed in the Savoy States at the time of Waterloo. It was based on the French Gendarmerie and its responsibilities and organisation remain similar to that ancient French body.

The *Carabinieri* does not regard the frontier with France as causing any particular problems, although its relations are probably better with its counterpart, the French *Gendarmerie*, than with the National Police, which has responsibility for policing France's border crossing points. It also feels that, complementary to the existing bilateral agreements, the Schengen accord will promote judicial collaboration on a reciprocal basis and that the existing three kilometre limit imposed on 'hot pursuit' will probably be increased to 10 or 15 before long.

Personnel posted to the frontiers receive special language tuition and should, therefore, be able to speak the appropriate language. However, members of the *Carabinieri* do not appear to be particularly proficient in foreign languages and, out of a total strength of nearly 100,000, only 1,276 (1.27%) speak any other language reasonably fluently. Of these, 432 (34%) speak German, 399 (31%) English, and 329 (26%) French. Only 101 (8%) speak Spanish and very few speak other languages. It is nevertheless estimated that some 15% in fact have a working knowledge of French or English, gained as a result of their schooling.

The extensive borders with Switzerland and Austria account for the comparatively high number of German-speakers but, although Italy has a border with Slovenia (Yugoslavia), only *one* member of the Carabinieri speaks fluent Slovene. Moreover, the French police officers on the Franco–Italian border hold the opinion that few of their Italian counterparts have any real knowledge of French and that, unless they use their own, somewhat limited knowledge of Italian, enquiries and messages often have to wait until a competent French speaker is available on the Italian side of the border.

In short, Italy may be compared with Spain and (possibly) Portugal as regards linguistic ability. The general level of knowledge of foreign languages in Italy is much lower than that in the northern countries, whether one considers the language(s) of neighbouring countries (France, Switzerland, Austria, Slovenia) or simply a knowledge of English which, as we have seen, is frequently employed as a convenient *lingua franca*. This national lack of linguistic ability is not surprisingly reflected in the Italian police forces and neither of the main forces can lay any real claim to competence in any foreign language. Moreover, there appear to be no indications that the authorities are taking seriously the need to train its police officers in other languages and it seems unlikely that the situation will improve in the foreseeable future.

Spain

The police service in Spain was completely reorganised in 1986 and there are now two national forces, the Civil Guard (*Guardia Civil*) and the National Police (*Cuerpo Nacional de Policia*), plus three autonomous 'community' police forces in the Basque country, in Catalonia and in Navarre. There are also numerous, fairly modest municipal forces which are mainly concerned with traffic control, the enforcement of bye-laws and similar matters in the larger towns.

For the sake of convenience only the two national forces have been surveyed. These follow largely the French system, with the National Police being responsible for policing urban areas and providing a criminal investigation service, while the gendarmerie-style Civil Guard is mainly concerned with the smaller towns and rural areas. It is the latter force which has had responsibility for controlling the frontiers.

As is so often the case, one cannot detect any desire for these forces to grow closer and they are in fact often quietly critical of each other. There is no routine contact with the various municipal forces (some of which, such as those in Madrid and Barcelona, are quite large) and there is no simple way of defining areas of responsibility. There is considerable overlap and it is not unusual for all three forces to be working virtually in sight of each other, possibly on connected events, but without any form of liaison or cooperation.

Spain suffers particular problems as a result of the large number of foreigners who live wholly or partially in that country and it is well-known that these include some notorious criminals who use the country as a refuge or as a base for their criminal activities. There is also a substantial influx of North Africans, many of whom only speak Arabic and are often involved in drugs dealing, prostitution or terrorism.

In common with most of their colleagues in the various European police forces, the Spanish police see the greatest obstacle to effective police cooperation as being the widely differing legal systems which obtain and the restrictions placed on policemen from one country acting on the territory of another, other than under stringent legal constraints. The Spanish authorities have, in fact, signed agreements with France and Portugal which permit a degree of cross-border activity but, in the case of criminal investigations, any action must be covered by an official letter of request to the relevant judicial authorities.

Obviously, the lack of a common language further aggravates these difficulties, especially at the central, or management level. At the level of the frontier controls and customs, it is claimed that this problem is not so acute, as most officers stationed on the French or Portuguese borders have at least a rudimentary knowledge of the appropriate language and are thus able to resolve any difficulties which might arise. This contention has not been tested empirically and could well prove somewhat exaggerated.

Unlike their colleagues in Northern Europe, the Spanish police are not normally accomplished linguists. In the Civil Guard, out of a strength of some 65,000 officers, NCOs and men, only a mere 256 (0.4%) have the equivalent of 'A-level' (*bachillerato*) or higher qualifications in modern languages, while the similarly sized National Police has only 260. A much larger number of National Police officers, however, (over 4,000 or some 6%) have what is described as an 'executive' (working) knowledge of foreign languages. It comes as no surprise to learn that, of all the admittedly few Spanish police officers who can claim some ability in a foreign language, most (+ 64%) speak French. What is somewhat surprising, however, is the fact that only about 8% of these can speak Portuguese, the language of one of its immediate neighbours which has close similarities with Spanish. English is the second strongest language with some 160 qualified speakers (30%) plus around 25% of those with a working knowledge of languages.

There is no formal requirement for personnel serving in the frontier regions to speak the language of the neighbouring country but, it is claimed, most of them do. Communications are often eased by the existence of a commonly-spoken language or dialect in the border areas. For example, in the northwest corner of Spain, some three million people speak a dialect of Portuguese known as Galician, while in the north-east, on both sides of the border with France, Catalan is spoken by about six million, including 250,000 in France and 40,000 in Andorra, where it is the main language spoken. The Catalan language is of the Romance family, closely related to the Provençal of Southern France. Although these languages are very much under threat and in danger of becoming mere curiosities or just an interesting patois, their continued existence obviously helps to smooth relations between countries where they exist on either side of a border. The correspondence from the Spanish police authorities made no reference to these minority languages, possibly because of the small number of speakers in their forces but, in view of the vital need for cross-border communication, the value of these as a *lingua franca* in some of the border areas is probably out of all proportion to the actual number of speakers.

Language training is only given to commissioned Civil Guard officers attending the Staff College (*Academia Especial*) although financial inducements are offered to other ranks who wish to learn languages on a personal basis. Such training naturally concentrates exclusively on the major European tongues and does not include any of the local languages mentioned in the preceding paragraph. The force has declared its intention to provide language training for all its personnel in order to improve their knowledge of foreign languages and it will be interesting to see whether this intent quickly becomes a reality, or whether it will be another case of *mañana*!

What is clear is that the level of linguistic competence in the Spanish police in general is considerably lower than that in the northern European countries we have looked at and makes the record of the British police forces seem a little less pathetic.

Portugal

With a population of only a little over 10 million, Portugal is one of the smaller Community countries. Although there are a large number of Portuguese speakers throughout the world, these are mostly to be found in Brazil or the former Portuguese colonies in Africa and Asia and the language is spoken by few outsiders in Europe, even natives of its immediate neighbour, Spain. In fact, Tamaron (1992) declares that Spain always ignores Portugal and Portugal erroneously believes that Spain wants to swallow it up.

As we have seen, few countries in continental Europe have just one police force and Portugal, despite its modest size, is no exception. Policing responsibilities are shared between:

(1) the Criminal Police (*Policia Judiciària*) which deals with serious crime.
(2) the Public Security Police (*Policia de Segurança Publica*), which polices the main urban areas, and is responsible for public order and air- and sea-port security;
(3) the National Republican Guard (*Guarda Nacional Republicana*), a gendarmerie-style force, responsible for policing the rural areas.

This division of responsibility owes more than a little to the fact that the country experienced a military coup as recently as 1974 and there is a natural reluctance to place too much power in the hands of any single body.

The Criminal Police has a strength of some 3,000 and is an entirely plain-clothes organisation, responsible to the Ministry of Justice for the prevention and detection of crime, especially the more serious offences. It is naturally concerned with international crime and incorporates the country's National Central Interpol Bureau. It has a central Violent Crime Squad which deals with mainly terrorist-inspired offences, a central Drugs Squad and a central Fraud Squad, as well as regional sections which deal with more local crimes.

The head of the Criminal Police is always a judge or public prosecutor and, since the Portuguese system is very similar that in France, the senior officers (*Commissarios*) are either law graduates or experienced detectives. Even the lower ranks are recruited from the better-educated echelons and therefore tend to have at least a smattering of English or Spanish which is of great assistance when pursuing enquiries in another country.

The *Policia de Segurança Publica* is a para-military force about 18,000 strong, commanded by serving army officers led by a General. It is responsible for public order and undertakes normal policing tasks in towns with more than 10,000 inhabitants, except the investigation of serious crimes, which are dealt with by the Criminal Police. It is also responsible for manning ambulances and policing harbours and airports, controlling arms and explosives and protecting VIPs.

Having a military two-tier entry system (officers and other ranks), the ability of members of this force to speak a foreign language depends to a large extent on the rank held. Commissioned officers will obviously have been selected from those with a higher level of education which will have included at least basic tuition in a foreign language. It will therefore not be difficult for these to communicate with their counterparts in Spain or, possibly using English as the *lingua franca*, the other EC countries. Where the lower ranks are concerned, this will not be the case and linguistic ability at this level tends to be very poor, although those working on or near the border often have a working knowledge of Spanish.

The other uniformed force, the GNR, has an authorised establishment of nearly 20,000 and is concerned with general policing, road traffic, public order and safety in the rural or semi-rural areas. The General in charge of the force believes, like most senior police officers in Europe, that terrorism, drug trafficking and organised crime will prove the biggest problems following the removal of border controls. He also anticipates a substantial increase in road traffic, all of which will lead to more work for the force.

Because of these problems, actual or anticipated, the GNR hierarchy maintains that the fundamental requirement will be for an international intelligence system to monitor terrorist organisations and organised crime, together with a suitable, computerised information system to ensure the prompt dispatch and receipt of essential intelligence. The force is of the view that there is no great benefit to be obtained from some monumental European data base but that access to the data bases held by the police forces in other countries should be the aim. In the light of this comment it has to be pointed out here that the Portuguese police have yet to be endowed with any sophisticated information technology systems and they are very much behind most of their European colleagues in this respect.

It is recognised that the lack of a common language makes the exchange of information and sharing of experience extremely difficult. One solution being adopted is the organisation of language courses embodying a student exchange system, coupled with the posting of liaison officers. Tentative arrangements have already been made with the Spanish authorities, with the object of gradually abolishing the border controls between the two countries. In order to prevent any loss of security resulting from the absence of border controls, it has been agreed that joint control points should be set up (like the French *commissariats mixtes*) with officers from both countries working hand-in-glove and using compatible communications systems. It is also planned to set up a mechanism for regular contacts and the organisation of joint activities, with regular meetings being held between police officers from both sides of the Spanish/Portuguese frontier.

There are reciprocal agreements for police surveillance and pursuit within the territory of each other's country for up to 50 km or for a period of two hours. The appropriate authority must be informed beforehand or, where this is not possible, as soon as possible, through the dedicated communications systems. 'Hot pursuit' is limited to cases of homicide or serious assault, kidnapping, drug and slave trafficking and breaches of the law relating to arms and explosives.

As has been previously mentioned, the Portuguese authorities agree that problems of comprehension do arise between the two countries because of the lack of a common language, especially among the lower ranks. It is claimed that most GNR personnel understand and speak Spanish quite well, especially those serving in the border areas. In view of the general level of language ability among the Portuguese this is a bold claim and not one which the writer has been able to test. Certainly, few Portuguese uniformed policemen (or policewomen) speak English or French, especially among the constable and sergeant ranks; the official response averred that the number was too small to record, despite the large number of tourists and other visitors from these two countries. In an effort to rectify this situation, the Portuguese police authorities have, for several years now, been tackling this problem by organising courses in these languages for (a) the traffic police and (b) sergeants and constables on general duties. This is not a result of the Schengen Accord or the Single Market but due to the specific nature of the GNR's duties. Tuition in both English and French has always been given on the more advanced courses at the Portuguese civil and military training establishments.

As is so often the case, relations between the various national police forces, although claimed to be excellent are, in point of fact, subject to the usual jealousies and rivalries. In particular, the Civil Police and GNP are fiercely proud of their history and reputation and regard themselves as a cut above each other and the much newer Criminal Police.

Summary

Although no hard and fast figures are available (and would, in fact, be very difficult to obtain), there seems to be clear evidence that, whilst most of the northern States in the European Community have an impressive mastery of foreign languages, this is not the case in countries such as France, Portugal and Italy — or at least not to the same degree. And such skills are virtually non-existent in Great Britain and in Spain.

Of course, the use of more than one language in a given area is not confined to the European Community. We have already noted that there are three official languages in Belgium and the same situation applies, to a greater or lesser degree, in certain other countries throughout the world. In the next chapter we will therefore take a look at three of these countries to see how the police there cope with this problem of multilinguality and examine whether the police forces of Europe might benefit from their experience.

7 Other Countries

In the first chapter of this book, our objective was declared to be an examination of the dispersion of linguistic skills throughout the European Community. But, of course, language problems are not confined to this disparate group of highly-autonomous nations; we have already noted that there are three official languages in Belgium (one being very much a minority one) and the same situation applies, to a certain extent, in Switzerland, Canada and South Africa. It seems it might therefore be useful to take a look at these countries to see whether one might detect some form of 'best practice' which could be applied to European Community policing.

Switzerland

The nearest neighbour to the European Community (and a candidate for future membership) is Switzerland, a confederation of 23 *cantons*, each of which is largely autonomous with its own police and judicial system. Indeed, in some respects, Switzerland may be looked upon as the European Community in microcosm, with all its historic, political, linguistic, economic and commercial hang-ups — even down to the federation/confederation dispute.

There is no Swiss language by which the Swiss people may be identified — or with which they can identify. There are no fewer than four official languages, of which only three are really in general use. Most of the Swiss (circa 65%) speak the curious Swiss-German dialect (Schwyzer Dütsch) — although the written language is normally High German — while some 18% are French-speaking and around 9% Italian-speaking. Only about 2% speak the fourth official language, Romansch. As a nation formed out of resistance to Austrian rule (readers will no doubt recall the stirring tale of William Tell's resistance to his Austrian overlords) and which successfully fought off takeover bids by Savoy, by France (during the Napoleonic Wars) and even by Adolf Hitler (who boasted he would take Switzerland with the Berlin fire brigade), Switzerland has built its considerable reputation on independence and neutrality, reinforced by a remarkable, highly-confidential banking system.

The Federal Constitution confers certain powers on the Confederation and others on the cantons. Apart from some minor crimes and non-criminal offences, the right to legislate on criminal matters is retained by the confederation. There is also a Federal law of criminal procedure to cater for the differences between Federal and Cantonal crimes.

The Swiss are generally good linguists, largely due to the fact that, under their system of education, pupils leaving school should be able to speak at least two languages. The first 'foreign' language (usually French or German, depending on the pupil's native tongue) is taught from the time of entering primary school at the age of seven. In the secondary schools, a second foreign language is introduced from the age of 11, tuition in the first foreign language continuing alongside this. Pupils who go on to a technical school continue to learn two foreign languages up to the age of 19 or 20, while those who move on to the *gymnasium* (grammar school) at the age of 13 immediately commence a third and a fourth foreign language, tuition in which continues until they leave school at the age of 17 or 18, usually to go on to university or polytechnic.

The typical Swiss police officer has usually served an apprenticeship and learned and practised a different, usually non-academic, profession for a few years before entering the police service. Perhaps as a consequence of this experience of other walks of life, the police have built up an enviable reputation for quiet, quasi-Teutonic efficiency. They are not particularly liked by the populace but they are demonstrably respected, as indeed are most forms of authority (unlike many countries these days). The higher ranks are often recruited directly from outside the police, drawn from suitable candidates with academic or legal qualifications.

In order to obtain a reasonably representative sample of the Swiss police, contact was made with the Swiss Federal Police, one French-speaking *canton* (Vaud), and one German-speaking *canton* (Berne). The Cantonal police forces are generally organised on a tripartite system; criminal investigation division, security (general) police, and traffic police. In the case of the French-speaking cantons, the latter two divisions are usually combined to form a *Gendarmerie*, while the criminal investigation division is usually referred to as the *Sûreté*. The ranks of the uniformed police generally follow the military system.

Swiss Federal Police

The small, Swiss Federal Police has the task of investigating offences likely to jeopardise the internal and external security of the Confederation, together with the gathering of intelligence concerning such offences. It also provides the National Interpol Bureau. Since the agents of the Federal Police deal mostly with serious offences against the nation as a whole (rather like the FBI in the US) they are investigative agents rather than uniformed law enforcement officers.

The view of the head of this force is that the problem of communication in Switzerland is marginal, since the average, educated Swiss knows two languages, usually French and German, at least on a reading or recognition level. As a rule, agents work in their *canton* of origin and the language skills of applicants for the force are taken into consideration when they apply. Most agents are competent in both French and German; the third vernacular — Italian — is not seen as very significant as the Federal Police agents working in such a *canton* will normally be native Italian speakers who are fluent in French and/or German as well.

As a rule, there is no need to provide any further linguistic training for Federal Police agents for the purpose of domestic communication and, since between them, they can speak the languages of their neighbours — Italy, France, Germany and Austria, there are few extra-frontier problems either.

Vaud

Much the same applies in the French-speaking canton of Vaud. According to the Commandant of the *Police Cantonale*, all candidates for the *Sûreté* (CID) must speak another of the national languages, preferably German. So far as the *Gendarmerie* is concerned, attachments and courses are arranged with other forces to help some of these uniformed officers to learn or improve their knowledge of German or Italian.

On the whole, therefore, the francophone members of the force are generally able to communicate in another (or both) of the official languages of the country, virtually eliminating linguistic difficulties.

Berne Police

Given the excellent schooling in languages received by all Swiss children, applicants for the Berne police are expected to be able to speak, read and write both German and French. The police training school provides additional opportunities to learn either Italian or English; 90% choose English. Consequently, one can reasonably anticipate that German-speaking officers, like those in this canton, will be bilingual in French and German, with possibly a good knowledge of English. As such, they share with their French-speaking compatriots the ability to communicate freely with most of their colleagues throughout Europe and even beyond.

General

The rules for communication between Swiss police forces stipulate that each should express itself in its own language. This particularly applies in the case of written documents: messages sent by Swiss-German forces are always in German while replies from a Swiss-French force will be in French. There are sufficient bilingual personnel on either side to ensure that this presents no great difficulties. On the whole there are no serious squabbles, petty rivalries or competition between forces due, no doubt, to the fact that, being organised geographically, their areas of competence do not overlap in any way. Cooperation between forces is well-established, both in principle and in practice.

Being accustomed to coping with this problem over the centuries and given that the number of official languages is limited to two or three, it is undoubtedly easier for a country such as Switzerland to find a solution to inter-force communications problems than it will be for the members of the European Community where language skills are, on the whole, less well-developed and the number of possible language combinations infinitely greater. However, the Swiss experience shows that it is indeed possible for police forces to understand each other relatively easily, especially where the education system of the country provides a good grounding in specific foreign languages.

South Africa

South Africa was originally settled by Dutch and French farmers (*boers*) but British settlers began to arrive in the 18th century and gradually displaced these early colonists. This situation led to a number of minor conflicts and, eventually to two full-scale wars in which the British were eventually triumphant. A degree of hostility still exists between the descendants of these early settlers, identified by the language they speak, although this pales into insignificance these days beside the antagonism of the black population who seek to gain control of the government of the country.

Today, the Republic of South Africa has a population of some 34 million who, for the historical reasons outlined above, use two official languages: English and Afrikaans, the latter being a development of the old Dutch language. The subsequent isolation of the people from their European homeland led to increasing deviations from the original Dutch so that Afrikaans is now considered to be a discrete language. There are, in addition, nine native tribal languages, of which Zulu and Xhosa are the most widespread, not to mention a great many dialects. The official policy behind the decision to make only English and Afrikaans the languages of the country is that it would be undesirable to use all these ethnic or tribal languages for internal communication as, apart from the logistical difficulties, it would promote sectarianism — a serious concern in a country with severe racial problems. Most black South Africans speak one of the tribal languages but those in the urban areas also have at least a working knowledge of one of the official languages.

So far as the whites and coloureds (persons of mixed race) are concerned, about 65% normally speak Afrikaans and 35% English. Proficiency in the official languages varies from person to person and so, in order to avoid ambiguity, the level of language employed in normal communication is kept to that which would be used at high school level. This fairly simple register is even used by academics in order to eliminate any possible misunderstanding or confusion.

At the time of the Boer War at end of the 19th century there were a number of independent urban and rural police forces in South Africa, including the Cape Mounted Police, the Transvaal Police, the Natal Police, the Orange River Colony Police, etc. These continued to exist even after the establishment of the Union of South Africa in 1910 and it was not until three years later that most of these existing forces were amalgamated into two main forces — the South African Police and the South African Mounted Riflemen. These two forces were themselves amalgamated in 1920 and, over the ensuing years, the few remaining borough forces, such as that in Durban, were similarly assimilated into the new South African Police.

In more recent times the South African Police have gained an unfortunate reputation for insensitivity and brutality due to their having to enforce some very unpopular *apartheid* policies and laws and their efforts to control a violent and rebellious black demographic majority. The force is multi-racial with about half its 40,000 members being white and the rest Blacks, Coloureds or Indians. It is also, since 1972, a mixed sex force, although the senior ranks tend to be reserved for white males with only a little over 1% of the commissioned ranks being held by non-Whites. It is organised on para-military lines and uses military ranks; indeed, fighting units formed from the force served with distinction in both World Wars. It is a prerequisite that all applicants for the force must be fluent in both official languages. This is demonstrated by the holding of a matriculation certificate (roughly 'O' level equivalent) which requires a pass in both English and Afrikaans.

In situations where an investigating or patrol officer is unable to communicate directly in a particular tribal language, the ethnic composition of the force is such that there is always a linguistically-capable policeman available to act as interpreter. In the more remote rural areas where a specific native language is predominant and the local population have less than a working knowledge of either of the official languages, members of the force who are versed in that particular tribal language are used to police the area or are assigned to accompany units operating in the area and act as interpreter.

As in the general life of the country, Afrikaans is the predominant language in the SA Police, but all regulations and standing orders are written in both English and Afrikaans.

By restricting the number of languages to just two, and thanks to the widespread teaching of both of these in the schools, most South Africans are bilingual and communication between the two groups presents no problems. In this respect, the force has a number of similarities with Belgium and Switzerland.

Canada

Like South Africa, Canada was first settled by other than English-speaking colonists, in this case the French. They founded a community on the coast of Nova Scotia and then sailed up the St Lawrence to what is now Quebec. British settlement started two years later on Newfoundland. These colonial initiatives expanded and the two great enemies took to destroying each other's settlements, recruiting the native Indian tribes as allies. These territorial disputes culminated in the Seven Years' War during which the British army routed the French and established British supremacy in the colony.

Despite this British military victory the country continued to support separate British and French cultures, languages and institutions. Since the number of French settlers in Quebec greatly outnumbered those of British descent, it was decided to retain French civil law and the French language in this province, a system which continues to this day. The number of British settlers increased during the American War of Independence as those American colonists who had no wish to become embroiled in the hostilities moved northwards. In addition, immigration from the Mother country was encouraged in the early 19th century, resulting in a predominance of English-speaking citizens. Despite this fact, the country continues to use two official languages and a census carried out in 1986 showed that, out of a total population of some 25 million, 73% spoke English as their first official language and 26% French.

Since 1969 both languages have enjoyed equal status in all Federal institutions, a position which is enshrined in the 1988 Official Languages Act. A survey made by the Official Languages Information System revealed that more than half the public service posts advertised demanded fluency in English while only 6.5% insisted on French. About one-third called for bilingual ability while the rest accepted either.

The use of these languages tends to polarise within certain provinces and, in this respect, Canada resembles Belgium or Switzerland rather than South Africa. The province of Quebec for example is primarily French-speaking while the other provinces tend to be predominantly English-speaking. Like Belgium, relations between the two linguistic sections is not always cordial and there is a strong separatist movement in Quebec. The anglophone Canadians in the rest of Canada are violently opposed to any suggestion of secession, if only for the reason given by Trofimov (1992) that '...bilingualism is the only thing which differentiates Canada from the United States and stops it from becoming the 51st state of the Union'.

Whatever the future might hold, for the time being at least the linguistically-different peoples of Canada have to co-exist, and that includes the police. Like most countries, there is one police force with nation-wide competence (the Royal Canadian Mounted Police — the 'Mounties' of story-book fame) — plus two Provincial forces (the Ontario Provincial Police and the Quebec Sûreté) and a number of city forces in the major urban centres of population (Toronto, Calgary, Montreal, Ottawa, Vancouver, etc.).

Outside those cities which have their own municipal force the two provincial forces are responsible for policing the whole of their respective provinces while the RCMP covers the remainder of the vast country, including the sparsely populated North-West Territories, the Yukon and the great prairie provinces of Alberta, Saskatchewan and Manitoba.

Despite having two official languages, Canadians are not generally bilingual, unlike for example the South Africans. So far as the francophone Canadians are concerned, the Quebec Sûreté points out that, being encircled by 260 million anglophones, they are accustomed to hearing English spoken, both on radio and TV and in the day-to-day contacts they have with the English-speaking population. Much of this, naturally, rubs off and, consequently, those police officers whose duties require them to communicate with the other provinces usually have a good knowledge of English. Where it becomes necessary for a non-English speaking member of the Quebec force to communicate regularly with his anglophone colleagues, he is given an intensive course in the language.

In Ontario, the largest anglophone province, the freedom to use French is recognised by the province's French Language Services Act of 1986. Being responsible for policing the greater part of Ontario, the Ontario Provincial Police (OPP) is faced with the challenge of providing a service in French, seven days a week, 24 hours a day in the areas designated by the Act. To achieve this it has formed a French Language Services Implementation Committee and appointed a coordinator of French Language Services. A coherent 3–5 year plan was produced which resulted in about 10% of all the posts in the OPP being designated bilingual.

One of the most important aspects of the OPP's implementation plan has been a large-scale language training programme including total immersion, part-time classes, one-to-one training for executives, correspondence courses and subsidies for personnel 'doing their own thing'. Being introduced in 1988 in the form of a five-year training programme, it will be considerably scaled down after 1993.

Bilingual OPP officers are generally posted to those areas which have the greatest number of French-speaking citizens. These are also the areas which have the most contact with the Quebec Sûreté, with which a reciprocal exchange programme is being negotiated. At present, as both forces have bilingual staff, communications between the two forces are officially conducted in either French or English (in practice more often than not in English).

As mentioned previously, while most of the larger cities have their own forces, only Quebec and Ontario have police forces covering the whole of the province and policing the remaining Canadian provinces, outside the major towns, is the responsibility of the Royal Canadian Mounted Police. Under the terms of the 1988 Official Languages Act, the RCMP is required to deal with the public, including victims, witnesses and accused persons, in the official language of their choice.

Of the 14,000 regular members of the RCMP, 83% are native English-speakers and only 17% are francophones. Some 15% can claim to be bilingual by virtue of having been officially tested in the other language. Where an officer is not fluent in both languages he is issued with a bilingual card expressing his inability to speak the other language and offering to contact someone who does:

I am sorry, I do not speak English. If you wish I will do everything possible to contact a person who does. If you agree with this proposal, point to this sentence.

Je regrette, je ne parle pas français. Si vous le désirez, je ferai tout mon possible pour contacter une personne qui le parle. Si vous êtes d'accord avec cette proposition, veuillez pointer cette phrase.

Similarly, personnel manning police telephones and switchboards have been given instructions on how to provide an 'active offer of service' in the form of cards giving basic responses in both languages. Where the operator is not bilingual, he/she has to connect callers as soon as possible to someone capable of speaking the required language, advising them (in the appropriate language) to hold the line.

To meet the demand for a bilingual response, so-called 'Unit Bilingual Complements' (UBCs) have been set up at the RCMP national headquarters in Ottawa and at 492 other 'places of significant demand'. It has been estimated that to man all these UBCs a total of 3,148 bilingual officers will be needed and, in September 1989, there were in fact 2,130 or 67%. This shortfall is not due to any failure on the part of the force to provide suitable and sufficient training but because of the lack of qualified, official testers and the unprecedented demand on their time as a result of the Official Languages Programme. To be classified as bilingual the member must have been tested within the past three years.

The linguistic capabilities of all personnel (police and civilian staff) are recorded on the force's PARADE computer system and it is claimed that the force's telecommunications system enables any member from any location in Canada to obtain assistance from a bilingual colleague at any time. In other words, assistance in either official language is only a telephone or radio call away.

All RCMP public notices are written in both languages, as are signs inside and outside police buildings. All RCMP publications are available either in bilingual format or in separate English and French versions, each bearing a note about the availability of the publication in the other language.

Under RCMP policy, all oral and written communications from the National Headquarters for general circulation throughout the force must be distributed simultaneously in both languages. Those addressed to C Division (Quebec) only must be either bilingual or, where the originator's written communication was in French, in that language. The RCMP has official translation offices in Regina, Toronto, Ottawa, Montreal and Fredericton which translate 6 million words each year, although other bilingual employees are encouraged to translate short, outgoing administrative documents (fewer than 500 words) from verbal or written notes. This ensures a more efficient use of the existing, official translation facilities and resources.

In 1988/89, the RCMP accepted 752 recruits, 200 of whom (27%) were already bilingual. Recruits who are not bilingual receive 200 hours training in the second official language while those showing ability to progress further receive an additional 800 hours. All members, police and civilian, have the opportunity to pursue their language studies to a higher level and each year about 125 do so. It is planned that the bilingual capability of all UBCs throughout the force will reach 90% by mid-1993.

All these initiatives are, as has been described, very recent and, given this sudden stimulus in language awareness, the greatest problem appears to be the shortage of adequate testing facilities for the many candidates wishing to take the Language Knowledge Examination.

Summary

In this and the preceding chapter we have looked at four multi-lingual countries, examining the education system in each as it affects language learning and the effect of this on police personnel. In all cases there are two main official languages of equal standing and, in some cases, other minor official languages. Only in Switzerland is the third language, in this case Italian, of any significant importance.

Perhaps the point which emerges most strongly in most (but not all) cases is the teaching of the second official language in the schools to a very high level. Only in Canada has this not been the case in the past, although the very recent initiatives inspired by the Official Languages Act looks set to alter this position.

What also emerges is the fact that, where the requirement is only for two languages, with a third being a possibility in some cases (Belgium, Switzerland), the educational system of a country is generally able to cope adequately, with the result that all school leavers at a certain, fairly moderate level, are able to communicate moderately well in at least one language other than their mother tongue. This ability is naturally reflected in the police which, drawing all or some of its recruits from a reasonably educated sector of the population, is usually able to claim a high level of bilinguality. Only in Canada is this not the case and a concerted effort is being made to rectify the situation, albeit only since it was made a mandatory requirement by legislation. Even here, the number of bilingual police personnel is growing very rapidly, despite any shortcomings in the general education system of the country. Nevertheless, an annual recruitment figure which includes 27% bilinguals is not bad going for any country.

The lesson to be learned from these countries therefore seems to be that, given a limited number of official languages, coupled with a progressive language learning ethic in the schools and elsewhere, it is possible for the vast majority of citizens, including the police, to communicate with each other with a degree of ease and fluency to be envied in many another country, especially in parts of Europe.

Apart from South Africa, where both the official languages are widely spoken in all parts of the country, the language dispersion tends to be restricted, in the main, to particular areas, such as the use of French in southern Belgium, in the western cantons of Switzerland and in the Canadian province of Quebec. As such, it is tenable to compare these linguistically-delineated areas with the sovereign states of Europe in which different languages are spoken. No single language dominates in these countries (at least, not in theory) and both or all the official languages have equal standing. Even where more than two languages are spoken, no single language overshadows the others to the extent that it has become regarded as a *lingua franca*, which tends to confirm the conviction that the common language solution is not really credible in the context of the European Community. All the evidence seems to point to the value of some form of international or cross-border bilinguality.

In all the cases cited, the police tend to have as their mother tongue the language of that part of the country in which they serve, speaking the language of the adjoining region as a necessity because of population movements. The high level of ability means that communication with both the public and with their police colleagues is therefore much more effective than would otherwise be the case.

8 Summary and Conclusions

> *If language is not correct, then what is said is not what is meant;*
> *if what is said is not what is meant, then what ought to be done*
> *remains undone; if this remains undone, morals and art deteriorate,*
> *justice will go astray;if justice goes astray, the people will stand about*
> *in helpless confusion.Hence there must be no arbitrariness in what*
> *is said. This matters above everything.* Confucius, ca.551–479 BC

The reader will recall that we started off by trying to establish the extent to which the absence of a common language is an obstacle to effective police collaboration in the Member States of the European Community. This question has been fully discussed in the preceding chapters and now, in this, the final chapter, we come to the point where an attempt is made to analyse the findings and draw some conclusions from them. As a result of this analysis it is hoped that we shall be in a position to evaluate the means by which the problems are being tackled in the various countries and to make suggestions as to how these difficulties might best be overcome or at least alleviated. In other words, does the research which has been carried out provide an indication as to any 'best practice' which might usefully be adopted by all or some of the countries concerned?

Post-1992 Problems

Almost without exception, the representatives of the various European police forces consulted agreed that cross-border problems of one sort or another did, in fact, exist and that these would probably be aggravated by the removal of border controls as a consequence of the Single European Act and the Schengen Accord. Indeed, according to Watson (1992) the impetus for one of the pillars of the somewhat ill-starred Maastricht Treaty is:

> ...the clear realisation that relaxing internal Community frontiers in the drive to the 1992 single market made cross-border cooperation more imperative to tackle a possible growth in international crime.

There is a surprising degree of agreement as to what the problems are, or will be. Virtually all the various police spokesmen expressed the view that the principal difficulties involve:

- the presence of different cultures;
- the lack of a common judicial system;
- an escalation in drugs trafficking, terrorism and organised crime;
- the absence of police powers in adjoining countries;
- the absence of a multi-national criminal intelligence system;
- the lack of a single language (where national borders coincided with a linguistic border);
- the general lack of language skills in some countries.

The first of these hurdles is probably gradually being overcome by a growing 'Europeanisation' of the citizens of the Member States. Although there is considerable resistance from the older inhabitants, there are encouraging signs that those in the younger age groups are increasingly seeing themselves as Europeans first and Germans, French, Italian or Dutch, etc. second. The greatest resistance to this phenomenon will probably come from the 'island' states, such as Great Britain, Ireland and Greece but, even here, it seems likely that the march towards Europeanisation will be inexorable.

The judicial problem is a very great one and also one for which there are no simple solutions. The great divide between the Common law countries and the Roman law countries is undoubtedly the biggest chasm to traverse, but there are wide differences between the various countries which are subject to a derivation of the Roman Law. Indeed, the German and American experience shows that there can even be significant differences between the various states within a single country.

These legal systems have evolved over the centuries. Common law was introduced in England by the Normans in an effort to rationalise the piecemeal Anglo-Saxon legal systems which existed at the time of the Conquest, while the Roman system, originating some two thousand years ago, was last radically reviewed by Napoleon in the early 19th century. Even in the thrusting, go-ahead United States, each State has its own system, that in Louisiana, for example, being based on the French model and consequently totally different to that in any other State. It would be foolhardy, therefore, to predict a sudden and cataclysmic sea-change in the legal systems of Europe following the creation of the European Community and the Single Market. Indeed, the experience of the United States lends credence to the view expressed by the House of Commons Home Affairs Committee that '...effective police cooperation does not require the laws of every member state to be identical...'. Nevertheless some degree of harmonisation is undoubtedly called for, as long as it is not what Alderson & Tupman (1990) describe as the German concept of harmonisation — everyone agreeing with their point of view!

This leads us on to the problems associated with drugs trafficking, terrorism and major crime — forms of criminality which have no common denominator in the national laws of the Member States. Drugs trafficking in the liberal Netherlands is not at all the same thing as drugs trafficking in much stricter Germany; terrorism is always problematical given that, to quote a popular cliché, one man's terrorist is another man's freedom fighter. As has already been mentioned, the fact that a country such as Libya, widely seen as encouraging and promoting terrorism, is a member of Interpol has been one of the major criticisms levelled against that body. The defining of certain, serious crimes as 'Euro crimes' remains a possibility but the task will be by no means an easy one.

In the comparatively recent past, law enforcement necessarily stopped at the national frontier and, unless a fleeing criminal was stopped by the border guards, he was able to obtain a measure of sanctuary in the adjoining country. Extradition was (and still is) a lengthy and uncertain process and the chance of getting off Scot-free very high. Whilst this has never been a great problem for a truly island State such as Great Britain or Ireland, the difficulties experienced by the authorities in the countries of mainland Europe can readily be appreciated.

The gradual introduction of various agreements, notably the formation of the Benelux group of nations and, more recently, the signing of the Schengen agreement, have done much to lessen this problem, and police generally have a degree of competence in the next country in urgent cases, although in these days of fast, reliable transport a limit of 10 km is almost ludicrous. Nevertheless, even where they are engaged in the hot pursuit of an offender, would any of us really wish to see foreign policemen operating freely in our own country? It will be necessary for the various police systems to have undergone a significant degree of harmonisation before this attitude changes.

The conducting of criminal investigations in foreign country is another matter which is currently exercising the minds of police and lawyers alike. The British system is such that there are few obstacles to this taking place, subject to the agreement of the local police but the Roman Law countries invariably require an international letter of request (*commission rogatoire*) to precede any such activity. This is not simply a case of the lawyers and judicial authorities in that country being pedantic or unduly difficult; it must be remembered that even the local police cannot conduct an investigation without a similar authority from the public prosecutor or examining magistrate. The letter of request is, in fact, the official document by which a public prosecutor or examining magistrate who has jurisdiction over a matter requests another magistrate or prosecutor or a police officer to carry out, or cause to be carried out on his behalf, one or more specific enquiries in connection with the preliminary proceedings before a court for which the delegating magistrate is acting. In most cases it is an examining magistrate who initiates such a request; in England and Wales it is now commonly the Crown Prosecution Service.

In this country, the letter of request has to be very precisely drawn up and then translated into the appropriate language before being passed to the Foreign & Commonwealth Office for dispatch in the diplomatic bag to the appropriate ministry via the British Embassy of the country concerned. It will be readily appreciated these formalities all take a long time and have to be completed before any investigation or enquiries are carried out. The possibility of the subject of the enquiry having moved on in the meantime is very strong, especially if he is a suspect rather than a witness. Some streamlining of the system is obviously an urgent requirement.

With the greatly enhanced ease of movement between countries afforded by the Single Market Act, the need to have knowledge of major or serious criminals becomes imperative. Most countries have a national system of criminal intelligence (as opposed to criminal records), usually computerised, although some, like Portugal, are not well-endowed in this respect. The problem arises when it is proposed to allow the police in other countries to have access to the national systems or else to establish a multinational system. Given the sensitive nature of criminal intelligence (which, by definition, will include hearsay and opinion as well as indisputable factual information), it is not surprising that efforts in this direction, such as the Schengen Information System, have met with considerable resistance. Data protection legislation differs widely from country to country and will have to undergo a considerable degree of *rapprochement* before any multinational criminal intelligence system can succeed. Interpol now has a computerised police information system which the National Central Bureaux can access direct and, in order to overcome this sensitive matter, access to particular items of information is restricted to those National Central Bureaux which the originating Bureau has specifically authorised to receive it. At the same time, the development of the Europol information system, being set up in Strasbourg, will be watched with a great deal of interest.

The question of international information systems brings us to the other difficulties referred to above — the lack of a single language and the paucity of language skills in some countries. Presumably any multinational criminal intelligence system which employs information technology will make extensive use of coded means of interrogation and response but one questions whether the use of free text can ever be totally eliminated. If this is indeed the case, what language(s) will be used?

All of which brings us full circle to the principal difficulties with which we are concerned and it will be recalled that, at the beginning of this book, three hypotheses were advanced:

(1) If there were a common language in use throughout Europe, senior police officers and other senior policy-makers would be better able to discuss international crime and common policing problems with their counterparts from other countries.

There seems little doubt that the findings expressed in the preceding chapters entirely support this hypothesis, although it is suggested (and accepted) that, at many of the types of conference referred to here, the crucial significance of the discussions makes it essential that professional interpreters are employed to ensure that there are no misunderstandings or ambiguity. Where there is a limited number of participating countries this is not a great obstacle (although it greatly increases the cost) but where all or most the nine languages of the Community are involved, the project takes on an altogether different dimension.

In practice, it is clear that English is frequently used as a *lingua franca* at meetings of personnel at all levels, especially where countries using more than two languages are concerned. Nevertheless, even in this sort of situation, a knowledge of other languages is seen as a definite advantage and helps to ensure that participants are not placed at an unfair advantage.

(2) That detective officers investigating crime or interviewing suspects or witnesses in other countries are hampered by their inability to speak the vernacular of the country concerned;

This contention too was supported by the research, although it may be that, as we have seen earlier, legal constraints, including the insistence on formal letters of request (*commissions rogatoires*) are, in most cases, the principal inhibiting factor. Unless and until the various countries in the European Community feel able to adopt a federal system of criminal law and procedure, this vital matter will continue to be a major obstacle to police efficiency.

However, even if agreement could be reached on a means of placing fewer or less severe restrictions on criminal investigations, the question of language will remain in many cases. Where it becomes necessary to make enquiries in another police area (even within the same country) there are basically two ways this can be accomplished. In some cases it may be sufficient merely to pass the relevant facts to the force covering that area with a request that an officer be permitted to make the necessary enquiry and forward the result to the enquiring force. This solution is widely used and not without considerable success but it has certain limitations, the main drawback being that the investigating officer has no means of pursuing a particular line of enquiry or posing supplementary questions. Thus, although suitable for obtaining statements from witnesses whose role is fairly clear cut, this method is of very limited value where the interviewee is a suspect. In such cases, the investigating officer needs to be able to adjust his questions to the responses he gets, to the body language of the suspect and a host of other factors which only someone present can take into consideration.

It is in circumstances of this nature that application has to be made to the host force or judicial authority for them to permit the investigating officer to travel to where the suspect or vital witness is to be found and continue his investigation there, usually in the presence of a local officer. Whilst this presents few problems within the United Kingdom, for example, in many other countries this will certainly call for a formal letter of request to precede the investigating officer or team. Such a letter will normally need to be accurately and professionally translated into the language concerned prior to dispatch through official channels if one is not to be exposed to the possibility of undue delay or unnecessary obstructiveness.

Armed with, or supported by, the previously accepted letter of request, the investigating officer duly travels to his destination where, in most cases, he will be received courteously and efficiently by his colleagues in the host force. But if the investigating officer is unable to speak the vernacular and the person to be interviewed does not speak the officer's own language, he immediately runs into problems. An interpreter will be needed which might be a member of the receiving force who happens to speak the officer's language fluently, a professional linguist who lives in the area and is introduced by the host force or, more unlikely but always a possibility, a police or other interpreter who has accompanied the investigating officer.

The efficacity of these solutions will depend on a number of factors, including the complexity of the case, the interpreter's knowledge of both languages and of police and court procedures and the investigating officer's ability to adapt to these strange circumstances. In any event, any meaning-ful dialogue will be subjected to the obstacle of an interface — the third party interpreter. Obviously this sort of situation must be seen as a second-best solution; nothing can match a direct, one-to-one confrontation in a language known intimately by both parties. What is abundantly clear is that a basic knowledge of the other person's language will be of inestimable assistance to the police officer conducting this sort of interview. Even if his command of the language is insufficient for him to conduct the interview in the interviewee's language, some knowledge of this, supported by a more expert assistant, will better enable him to detect hesitance, procrastination, deviation and other ploys, as well as help him match responses with the manner in which the questions are put.

Since one cannot expect all suspects or witnesses to speak a common language, whatever that language might be, it is evident that investigating officers will usually have to conduct their interviews in the interviewee's language. This concept is one which, as we have seen, Belgium has already embraced with its statutory policy that statements may be made in any language spoken by the witness or suspect. In practice, unless the witness is permitted simply to write his/her own statement in the preferred language, the police officer has either to be fluent in the interviewee's language or must rely on a third party, in which case a nodding acquaintance with the language concerned would be very helpful.

Taking the United Kingdom as an example, the ideal solution would be for each force to have a range of highly experienced detectives fluent in or well acquainted with all the languages of the European Community. Since this is an obvious non-starter, an alternative might be a national European Investigation Unit, composed of such officers, who could be called in by any British force to take over this particular aspect of any enquiry. The other possibility, a team of experienced, professional interpreters, willing and able to travel to anywhere in Europe at the drop of a hat to accompany an investigating team would certainly be too cumbersome and costly.

Failing the implementation of any of these suggested solutions, it will continue to be necessary for the police to rely on the cooperation of the host force and the use of its own in-house or external linguists, with all the inherent weaknesses of this system.

(3) If officers working on or near national frontiers used a common language, or could speak the language(s) of the adjacent country/countries, communication with (a) their colleagues across the border in emergencies and on everyday policing matters, and (b) foreign nationals visiting their country who have committed offences there or have become victims of crime, or who otherwise seek assistance, would be greatly improved.

This premise, too, was found to be fully justified and highly relevant. What may be described as the tertiary level of policing (or, if you prefer, the primary level since it is the most practical!) involves probably the greatest number of policing practitioners and the widest spectrum of police work.

It breaks down into two distinct sectors: border police and the police in the border regions and other tourist areas. The main difference lies in the fact that the former have traditionally been concerned with persons and vehicles crossing their particular border and, in most countries outside the United Kingdom, immigration matters. The second sector includes all those 'normal' police men and women who happen to be working in a town or village close to a national border or which attracts a significant number of foreign tourists. The latter category also includes police forces involved in the transport of tourists, such as traffic patrols and the British Transport Police. They are not involved in checking visitors to the country but will be involved where these commit offences, are offended against or need some form of assistance.

The virtual removal of the internal borders within the European Community means that most of the traditional functions associated with border police units will henceforth be confined to the external borders, airports and seaports. Their role on internal borders, if any, will tend to be transformed to one of liaison with the police in the adjoining country. Alternatively, they may be used to form roving, mobile intervention units, working in the general area of the border and concentrating on drug smuggling and similar cross-border crime. This is certainly a solution which several Customs services are adopting, since they too have become superfluous on internal borders.

It is reasonable to assume that, given much freer movement throughout the Community, the number of foreigners in any country will increase dramatically, whether in the guise of tourists, day-trippers, workers, job-seekers, students or, of course, criminals. The traders in London's Oxford Street are only too well aware of the teams of criminals who commit wholesale shoplifting offences in their stores. The majority of these are from abroad, and it is not unreasonable to anticipate that this sort of enterprise will become a growth industry, especially where a highly-developed country adjoins a less-developed one.

Where national frontiers are contiguous with linguistic borders there will necessarily be an increase in language-related problems. However, this increase will be just that — an increase. It will not be an entirely new phenomenon since there has always been a considerable amount of movement across national borders. Large numbers of French citizens (known as *frontaliers*) cross into Switzerland each day to work, Spaniards travel regularly to Biarritz, Germans regularly drive into Strasbourg, and so on. As we have seen, since the police in these border areas are often indigenous to the area and are well-acquainted with their neighbours, they often have a correspondingly sound knowledge of the language and culture of the other country. This is not always the case, however, and ability varies considerably, depending on the countries concerned.

Taking all the hypotheses outlined above, it is clear that the relevant police forces consulted were, for the most part (a) aware of the difficulties and (b) taking steps to alleviate them. The degree of awareness demonstrated by the various forces differed significantly, as do the steps being taken to overcome the difficulties.

Methodology

Having confirmed that there were indeed problems stemming from the absence of a single language, an attempt was made to analyse the these, using the tried and tested 'dependent/independent variable' type of analysis as proposed by Robson (1973). In doing so, the *independent variable* emerges as the level of linguistic ability in the various European police forces and the *dependent variable* the extent to which this affects cross-border cooperation. However, the nature of these is such that, in practice, they can only be measured qualitatively and so the application of X^2 techniques is problematic. Furthermore, as Table 8.1 contains an excessive number of 'empty cells', this violates the assumptions of that test.

Definitions

The level of linguistic ability was originally set at university entrance standard (e.g. 'A' levels, baccalaureate) and it was details of the number of officers with this level of linguistic skill which were sought from the various police forces. In the event, the numbers with this sort of qualification often proved to be so small that other criteria had to be employed. In any case, various correspondents laid considerable stress on the need for an adequate level of oral communication — something which academic qualifications do not necessarily confer, especially in a highly-specialised field such as police work.

The four levels which emanated may be described as (a) basic knowledge, (b) working knowledge (+ O-level), (c) good communicative ability (+ A-level), and (d) fluency (degree level or beyond).

It is equally difficult to define 'cross-border cooperation' and no bench mark exists to test the level of (or, indeed, the need for) such collaboration. In the past, for example, there has been much less call for the police in the UK to cooperate with their continental colleagues than there has been for the latter to collaborate with each other, especially where they share extensive land borders. It must be acknowledged and accepted, therefore, that the measurement will be entirely subjective, with all the ensuing possibility of bias.

Levels of Linguistic Competence

Enormous differences are evident in the linguistic abilities possessed by members of the various police forces, although it is clear that these tend to follow closely the national levels of linguistic competence. Thus, the police in the highly articulate Netherlands and in Belgium scored highly, whilst those in the UK and in the Iberian peninsular performed much less dramatically in this field.

The percentage of the population with a working knowledge of foreign languages is indicated in Table 8.1. This has been adjusted to reflect the figures as they apply to the police, where reliable information on such statistics has been obtained. However, in the absence of any accurate data, these figures must be seen as somewhat arbitrary and possibly biased.

Table 8.1 Estimated percentage of police with working knowledge of other languages

Country	Language							
	Eng	Fr	Ger	Dan	Dut	It	Sp	Por
GB	-	6	2	0	0	0	1	0
F	25	-	6	0	0	8	10	0
D	65	15	-	0	0	0	0	0
DK	85	10	70	-	5	0	0	0
NL	98	5	60	0	-	0	0	0
B	55	90	10	0	70	0	0	0
I	15	15	1	0	0	-	0	0
E	3	5	0	0	0	0	-	1
P	15	10	0	0	0	0	50	-
CH	20	75	80	0	0	20	0	0

Switzerland is included for the purposes of comparison.

The research has demonstrated that there are three essential ways in which police personnel (and others) acquire competence in a second (or additional) language:

(1) through the country's educational system'
(2) through post-school, vocational training, and
(3) a combination of the two.

In a few cases, such as the widespread use of German in Alsace and Lorraine, second languages are acquired as a result of historical or geographical accidents.

Table 8.2 Language(s) of cross-border cooperation

Border	Cross-border language	Shared language?
France/Belgium(Flanders)	French	No
France/Belgium(Wallonia)	French	Yes
France/Germany	German	No
France/Italy	French/Italian	No
France/Spain	French/Spanish	No
Spain/Portugal	Spanish	No
Belgium/Netherlands	Dutch	Yes
Belgium/Germany	German	Yes (part)
Netherlands/Germany	German	No
Denmark/Germany	German/English	No
England/France	English/French	No
England/Belgium(Flanders)	English	No

In most cases languages are learned at school and occasionally topped-up by vocational courses. Only in rare and specific cases were languages acquired entirely by a form of post-school education. This latter solution is obviously a much more time-consuming and expensive one and explains why the police in those countries where foreign languages are not widely taught in the schools (such as Great Britain) are generally linguistically ignorant. Unfortunately, it has to be recognised that, unless there is a significant change in the extent foreign languages are taught in our schools, we shall remain impoverished in this respect.

Having established the linguistic competence of the police in the various countries, the next stage was to determine which languages are used for cross-border collaboration. The results are shown in Table 8.2.

It will be noted that no single language stands out as a *lingua franca* — not even English, although it must be admitted that this is used on occasions by non-native speakers of English as a convenient means of communication. The inference therefore is that the concept of a *lingua franca* must give way to that of cross-border bilingualism — or at least the acceptance of a limited number of tongues as the working languages of the Community.

Interpol has gone down this road by nominating three working languages — French, English and Spanish — with Arabic being used during General Assembly sessions and as a working language within the General

Secretariat. At General Assembly meetings, any delegate may speak in another language, provided he makes arrangements for the interpretation of his speeches into one of the working languages. The attraction of this sort of solution is that all communications between Member States (of which there are 158) are in one of these three languages, thus reducing the translation and interpretation requirements to manageable proportions. As each country has to nominate a single office to act as its Interpol National Central Bureau, all necessary linguists can be concentrated there.

The tried and tested linguistic structure of Interpol therefore reflects the concept of national cross-border liaison units, the big difference being the fact that the Interpol Member States have agreed to use just three languages for normal working relations. Were the European Community to make a similar decision, a great deal of the problems we have been discussing would be resolved. Unfortunately, there are no signs of this happening at present, although future admissions to the Community may make it necessary to limit the number of working languages if it is not to imitate the Tower of Babel and collapse under the weight of its own bureaucracy.

Until this contingency arises, therefore, the police will have to concentrate on some form of local or frontier liaison unit, the members of which are able to speak the language(s) of the countries with which they are most likely to have dealings. Indeed, there would be little point in trying to insist, for example, upon Portuguese police officers liaising with their Spanish counterparts in (say) English or French. Effective cross-border cooperation must depend on use of at least one of the languages used either side of the border.

Cooperation

Having established the levels of linguistic competence and determined which languages are actually used for cross-border communication, the next task was to ascertain the extent to which these were related to the degree of cross-border cooperation which exists. Again, the scoring allocated to the various countries is arbitrary and subjective and should be treated with caution.

It will be seen from Table 8.3 that cross-border 'best practice' is exemplified by France/Flanders, France/Germany and Denmark/Germany, with Spain/Portugal, Germany/The Netherlands and Germany/Belgium close behind. Reference back to Table 8.2 shows that, only in the last case is the same language shared and then only partially (the small, German-speaking enclave in Belgium). To determine why these particular countries have such good cross-border relations we must look at each country in turn.

Table 8.3 Degree of cross-border cooperation

Border	Level of cooperation (points out of 5)	Notes
France/Belgium(Flanders)	5	
France/Belgium (Wallonia)	3	(1)
France/Germany	5	
France/Italy	2	(1)
France/Spain	3	(1)
Spain/Portugal	4	
Belgium/Netherlands	3	(2)
Belgium/Germany	4	
Netherlands/Germany	4	
Denmark/Germany	5	
England/France	3	(1)(2)(3)
England/Belgium	3	(1)(2)(3)

(1) Level of cooperation is limited by the lack of reliable contacts and adequate bilateral arrangements.
(2) Lack of a single national police force and/or inter-force rivalries have proved a hindrance to good cross-border liaison — e.g. police v *gendarmerie*.
(3) Wide differences in judicial processes have proved a substantial obstacle to close collaboration.

Germany stands out in that, despite having only a limited ability in languages apart from English, all its contacts merit a score of four or five. On three of the four European Community borders (Denmark, The Netherlands, Belgium), this may be mainly attributable to the fact that, in the neighbouring countries, the same or similar languages are spoken and these countries also all have a high standard of education and/or an advanced language training system, coupled with a well-developed language learning ethic. Only on the French border is a completely different language spoken and the success of the relations here must be attributed to hard work and the determination demonstrated on both sides of the border to establish sound liaison, plus the willingness of the French to use the German language where necessary. It would seem that the ability of the French to speak German is, for historical reasons as we have seen, greater than the ability of the Germans to speak French but even this is changing with the concentrated effort being made by the various German police forces which border on to France to teach their personnel to speak French. There is no doubt that relations on both sides of the border are extremely good and cooperation very close, this being buttressed by the various exchange programmes which have been prepared.

France does not have a particularly good reputation for speaking foreign languages and its success on the Belgian (Flanders) border must be attributed to the proficiency of the Belgians in French. Few Frenchmen in the Nord/Pas-de-Calais region show any particular proficiency in Dutch (although many of them speak quite good English). On the German border, however, it is the ability of the French Alsatians to speak German which is the crucial factor, although as mentioned in the last paragraph, the Germans are taking steps to improve their knowledge of French and this must not be overlooked.

It will not have escaped the reader's notice that, on France's borders with the other countries in which language skills are less evident (Italy, Spain, England), collaboration is less effective, although the French nation in general and the police in particular are making considerable efforts to improve their competence in these other languages.

It will be seen, therefore, that the success of the liaison on the borders of Holland, Belgium and Denmark with Germany depends to a very large extent on the ability of the police in these former countries to speak German (although English is occasionally used as a *lingua franca*). They also have the advantage of speaking German or a Germanic language which has close similarities with German.

The comparatively poor record of the inhabitants of the Iberian peninsular in speaking foreign languages has already been noted and, on the Spanish/Portuguese border, successful relations rely to a large extent on the willingness and ability of the Portuguese police to speak Spanish, especially in the border areas. The lack of ability on the part of the Spanish police to speak Portuguese does appear rather surprising.

The apparent lack of cooperation on the Dutch/Belgian border, where the police share a common language, is worthy of note and, according to Van Reenen (1989) may be attributed to inter-force rather than inter-nation rivalries. Similarly, relations between the French police and the French-speaking Belgian Walloons are curiously not as good as those with the Flemish speakers in North Belgium, although this may be due to questions of personality and lack of real commitment rather than any linguistic or legal obstacles.

Cross-border relations between the RCMP in Canada and the FBI in the United States, two countries and two police forces which share the same language, are reported to be excellent but reservations have to be expressed concerning the cooperation at other levels and between other forces. It is a well-known fact that, despite the fact that they share the same language and, to a certain extent, the same judicial and legal systems, there is great rivalry between the various city, state and county forces in the United States, occasionally resulting in obstructiveness and total lack of cooperation. In Canada, the geographical split between the areas covered by the RCMP and that covered by the provincial police forces, and between these and the various City police forces, undoubtedly goes a long way to ensuring that there is no treading on each other's toes.

The example shown by the police officers working on the Franco/German border shows that, provided those who are directly involved in cross-border liaison can speak each other's language reasonably well, cooperation does *not* necessarily call for a universally high skill in languages throughout the force, or for the nation as a whole to have a highly-developed language learning ethos. Only a very limited number of French police officers can speak German and, similarly, few of the Germans can speak French; it is the essential core of linguistically competent officers in the border areas which matters.

There are huge advantages to be gained where, in the country as a whole, languages are given a high profile in the general school curriculum, and/or there is a highly-developed vocational language training system. This is usually associated with a well-developed language learning policy as exemplified in the Scandinavian countries, the Netherlands, Belgium, Switzerland, etc.

It is evident that factors such as environment and culture play an insignificant role. The environment changes but little across the terrestrial borders, although admittedly the national cultures do show a more obvious change. Nevertheless, these factors appear to have only a minimal effect on the levels of collaboration and the statistical inference is that it is the level of linguistic ability possessed by a hard-core of police officers on one or both sides of a border which actually has the most substantial effect on trans-frontier cooperation.

Tackling the Problem

We commenced this study with the assumption that forces were aware of the problems posed by the lack of a common language and were taking steps to tackle these. Accordingly, an integral part of the study was to examine and evaluate the steps which were being taken to improve cross-border collaboration by improving linguistic skills.

As was to be expected, the research revealed that the measures taken varied widely, from country to country and from force to force within the same country (the latter being very much the case in the United Kingdom). From the foregoing analysis it will be seen that, where considerable emphasis is placed on second or other languages in the schools (The Netherlands, Denmark, Belgium, Switzerland, South Africa), the police (and other professions) merely need to 'top-up' these skills and convert the vocabulary to the specifics required for the job. Where less emphasis is placed on the subject in the schools or where schools tend to concentrate on the learning of English (France, Germany, Spain, Italy), it becomes necessary to fill the gaps with some form of subsequent, vocational language training and this is obviously an uphill and time-consuming task. In the case of the United Kingdom, with its abysmal record of foreign language teaching in its schools, the task is truly formidable.

Where police recruits lack an adequate level of language skills, it is not practical to inculcate such skills within the service other than in the case of a few, specific posts. The cost, in both time and money, which the training of all police officers in other languages would involve, the constantly changing needs, the difficulty in maintaining levels of competence and the varying levels of ability and motivation, all militate against such a solution.

The answer in such cases has to be, firstly, to provide suitable, intensive training for clearly identified personnel engaged on specialist duties on or near the borders and to ensure that the maximum use is made of these expensively trained officers. Secondly, the creation of readily available, bi- or multi-lingual liaison units, whether single-nationality formations of the type established in Canada and in Kent, or mixed-force units such as those to be found on the French/Belgian and French/German borders, is probably the most effective and efficient use of valuable resources.

The growth of bilateral arrangements and an increased understanding of each other's methods, organisation and procedures will in no way diminish the role of Interpol nor the possible creation of some form of European federal police force in the foreseeable future. However, these close and direct cross-border links will become increasingly important. The posting of individual officers to other countries has a real but limited value, due to the cost involved and the limitations on acceptable caseloads.

In the United Kingdom in particular, where linguistically able officers are thin on the ground, they should be recognised as a valuable resource and the maximum use made of these scarce talents. In the very near future, forces will be obliged to give serious consideration to posting them to areas or on duties where this ability can best be utilised, as in Canada, for example.

There will also be a growing need for bi- or multi-lingual documentation, of the type used in Canada, Belgium and that proposed by the British Transport Police. The Swiss practice of sending all communications in the originator's language is less attractive to European Community police forces in view of the large number of languages used (how quickly could the Portuguese police translate a document in Danish, or the Italian carabinieri one in Dutch?). Some use will continue to be made of external linguists, but these can be expensive and great care must be taken in their recruitment and training.

Finally, the use of dedicated machine translation systems for clearly-defined tasks (of which policing the Channel Tunnel is a prime example) may be viewed as an important policing tool for the future.

The police have had to learn and assimilate many skills throughout their history and, as we approach the second millennium, the concept of greater ease of travel and more sophisticated criminal methods will call for even greater attention to new methods and the learning of new skills. Certainly, so far as many of the police forces of Europe are concerned, linguistic skills have hitherto been very low down on the list of priorities but the indications are that this is rapidly changing and there will need to be a sweeping change in the attitudes adopted by at least some of the Member States of the European Community in this respect.

Appendices 1, 2, 3 and 4

Responses by British police forces to the questions posed.

Note 1: The following forces expressed their inability to assist in the research due to operational pressures :

Derbyshire

Lancashire

Leicestershire

Northumbria

Surrey

West Midlands.

Note 2: No response whatsoever was received from Gloucestershire and Warwickshire.

Note 3: The following forces referred the enquiry to the Association of Chief Police Officers (ACPO):

North Wales

South Wales

Staffordshire

Sussex.

Appendix 1

Responses by British Police Forces to Question 1: Problems Arising from Fact that Other Police Forces in Europe Speak Different Languages

Key to table opposite

1. Raises need for effective cooperation
2. Judicial differences paramount
3. Joint operations difficult
4. Difficulty in communicating information
5. No particular problems anticipated
6. Creates need for care in expression
7. Depends on country
8. Depends on level of interchange
9. Possibility of confrontations with foreigners
10. Local ethnic minorities more a problem
11. Problems need to be addressed in the schools
12. Need to become less xenophobic
13. Common use of English removes difficulties for general policing
14. Increasing need for professional linguists
15. Essential to build up cooperation with European forces
16. Mostly in documentation
17. Increased tourism/road traffic
18. Need to understand the ethics, politics and organisation of other forces

	1	2	3	4	5	6	7	8	9	10	11	12	13	14	15	16	17	18
Avon & Somerset	*																	
Bedfordshire		*	*	*														
Cambridgeshire					*													
Cheshire		*																
Cleveland					*													
Cumbria					*													
Devon & Cornwall						*												
Dorset								*	*	*								
Durham		*																
Dyfed Powys					*													
Essex									*									
G. Manchester					*					*								
Gwent		*			*													
Hampshire		*			*													
Hertfordshire		*																
Humberside					*													
Kent		*	*													*	*	*
Lincolnshire		*			*							*						
Merseyside					*													
Metropolitan		*			*													*
Norfolk	*													*		*		
Northants.	*														*			
N. Yorkshire																*		
Nottinghamshire					*													
S. Yorkshire																		*
Suffolk					*													
Thames Valley					*													
West Mercia			*	*														
W. Yorkshire					*													
Wiltshire											*							
Strathclyde					*													
Loth. & Borders					*													
Dumfries & Gall.																		*
RUC					*													
BTP				*				*	*							*	*	
Dover Harbour				*					*								*	
ACPO	*	*	*	*			*				*		*		*		*	

| | 1 | 2 | 3 | 4 | 5 | 6 | 7 | 8 | 9 | 10 | 11 | 12 | 13 | 14 | 15 | 16 | 17 | 18 |

Appendix 2

Responses by British Police Forces to Question 2: Do You See These Problems Increasing Post-1992?

Key to table opposite

1. Yes
2. No
3. Gradual process

	1	2	3
Avon & Somerset			*
Bedfordshire			*
Cambridgeshire		*	
Cheshire			*
Cleveland		*	
Cumbria		*	
Devon & Cornwall	*		
Dorset	*		
Durham	*		
Dyfed Powys		*	
Essex		*	
G. Manchester			*
Gwent		*	
Hampshire		*	
Hertfordshire		*	
Humberside			*
Kent	*		
Lincolnshire			*
Merseyside			*
Metropolitan	*		
Norfolk			*
Northants.			*
N. Yorkshire			*
Nottinghamshire	*		
S. Yorkshire	*		
Suffolk			
Thames Valley		*	
West Mercia	*		
W. Yorkshire	*		
Wiltshire	*		
Strathclyde		*	
Loth. & Borders		*	
Dumfries & Gall.			*
RUC		*	
BTP	*		
Dover Harbour	*		
ACPO	*		
	1	2	3

Appendix 3

Responses by British Police Forces to Question 3:
Will Accords Such as Schengen Add to These Problems?

	Yes	No
Avon & Somerset		*
Bedfordshire	*	
Cambridgeshire		
Cheshire	*	
Cleveland	*	
Cumbria		*
Devon & Cornwall	*	
Dorset		*
Durham		
Dyfed Powys		
Essex		*
G. Manchester		
Gwent		
Hampshire		
Hertfordshire	*	
Humberside	*	
Kent		
Lincolnshire		*
Merseyside		
Metropolitan	*	
Norfolk		*
Northants.		
N. Yorkshire		
Nottinghamshire	*	
S. Yorkshire	*	
Suffolk		
Thames Valley		
West Mercia	*	
W. Yorkshire	*	
Wiltshire	*	
Strathclyde		*
Loth. & Borders		
Dumfries & Gall.		
RUC		*
BTP		
Dover Harbour		
ACPO		

Appendix 4

Responses by British Police Forces to Question 4: What Steps are Being Taken to Alleviate the Problem?

Key to table opposite

1. None
2. Encouragement for all or some officers to learn in own time
3. Distance learning courses provided
4. Part-time courses provided for key staff
5. Full-time/residential courses provided for key staff
6. Courses/visits abroad arranged
7. Exchanges with other forces arranged
8. Recourse to interpreter list (police & others)
9. Phrase book in use/under consideration
10. Use of 'Language Line'
11. No general training provided
12. Language audits carried out
13. Training confined to native/ethnic languages
14. Linguists actively recruited
15. Conversation groups
16. Machine translation initiatives

	1	2	3	4	5	6	7	8	9	10	11	12	13	14	15	16
Avon & Somerset			*					*	*							
Bedfordshire		*						*		*						
Cambridgeshire		*						*								
Cheshire								*				*				
Cleveland		*						*								
Cumbria		*						*								
Devon & Cornwall				*	*							*				
Dorset	No details supplied															
Durham												*				
Dyfed Powys													*			
Essex		*				*		*				*				
G. Manchester	*															
Gwent								*				*				
Hampshire					*			*								
Hertfordshire								*		*	*					
Humberside	*															
Kent		*		*	*	*	*	*						*		*
Lincolnshire		*														
Merseyside		*			*	*										
Metropolitan		*			*						*					
Norfolk				*				*	*							
Northants.		*		*												
N. Wales													*			
N. Yorkshire		*						*								
Nottinghamshire		*					*	*			*					
S. Wales	*							*								
S. Yorkshire				*		*		*							*	*
Suffolk		*						*								
Sussex		*		*							*	*				
Thames Valley	*							*								
West Mercia				*					*							
W. Yorkshire	*							*								
Wiltshire			*	*				*	*							
Strathclyde												*				
Loth. & Borders		*						*								
Dumfries & Gall.	No details received															
RUC		*										*				
BTP				*		*		*								
Dover Harbour		*						*								
ACPO							*		*		*					*
	1	2	3	4	5	6	7	8	9	10	11	12	13	14	15	16

References

Alderson, J.C. (1989) 1992: Are border controls necessary? *Police Journal*, July 1989, 240.

Alderson, J. and Tupman, W. (1990) *Policing Europe After 1992*. Exeter: University of Exeter.

Anderson, M. (1989) *Policing the World*. Oxford: Oxford University Press.

Baker, D. (1989) *Language Testing*. London: Edward Arnold.

Baker, K. (1991) Police Foundation Lecture. Reported in *Police Review* 28 June, 1301.

Baker, S.R. (1988) When boundaries disappear. *Policing* 4 (4), 289.

Bartsch, H.J. (1989) Jurisdictional conflict. In J.C. Alderson and W.A. Tupman (eds) *Policing Europe After 1992*. Exeter: University of Exeter.

Bayley, D.H. (1975) The police and political development in Europe. In C. Tilly (ed.) *The Formation of National State in Western Europe*. Princeton: Princeton University Press.

Bell, C. and Norris, D. (1991) Europe backs English for all. *Daily Mail* 15 November.

Benn, T. (1991) The Commonwealth of Britain bill: How it would work. *The Independent* 11 July.

Binyon, M. (1989) Europe takes a tongue lashing, Part 1: How Europe fell. *The Times* 23 October.

Birch, Sir R. (1989a) Preparing for 1992. *Police Review* 17 February, 337

— (1989b) Policing Europe in 1992. *Policing* July, 204–9.

— (1990) Law Enforcement in Europe After 1992. Transcript of presentation given to 8th Annual European Chapter, National Academy Associates Retraining Session, September 1990.

Bittner, E. (1970) *The Functions of the Police in Modern Society*. Maryland: Chevy Chase.

Brittan, Sir L. (1991) Newsam Memorial Lecture at the Police Staff College, Bramshill.

Brumfit, C.J. and Roberts, J.T. (1983) *Introduction to Language and Language Teaching*. London: Batsford.

Cain, M. (1973) *Society and the Policeman's Role*. London: Routledge.

Canning, D. (1990) *Policing Europe Towards 1992*. Exeter: Devon & Cornwall Constabulary.

Carroll, L. (1865) *Alice in Wonderland*. London: Macmillan.

Chomsky, N. (1979) *Language and Responsibility*. Hassocks: Harvester Press.

Clutterbuck, R. (1990) *Terrorism, Drugs and Crime in Europe After 1992*. London: Routledge.

Colman, A.H. and Gorman, L.P. (1982) Conservatism, dogmatism and authoritarianism in British police officers. *Sociology* 16, 32.

Cross, J.P. (1991) Language and Empire. *The Linguist* 30 (2), 56.

Crystal, D. (1987) *Cambridge Encyclopedia of Language.* Cambridge: Cambridge University Press.

Deth, Van, J-P. (1989) 1993: Will it lead to an explosion in the language market? *Language International* 1 (3), 8.

European Businessman Readership Survey (1984) Quoted in *Language International* 3 (4), 6.

European Commission (1985) White Paper. Brussels, Commission of the European Communities, Point 24.

Field, A. (1985) *International Air Traffic Control.* Oxford: Pergamon Press.

Fortier, d'I. (1989) Interview reported in *Language International* 1 (4), 11.

Government (H.M.) (1991) *Response to the Home Affairs Committee's Report on Practical Police Co-operation in the European Community* (HC 363). London: HMSO.

Hamers, J.F. (1981) Psychological approaches to the development of bilinguality. In H. Baetens Beardsmore (ed.) *Elements of Bilingual Theory.* Brussels: Vrije Universiteit te Brussel.

Hamers, J.F. and Blanc, M.H.A. (1989) *Bilinguality and Bilingualism.* Cambridge: Cambridge University Press.

Harzic, J. (1976) Le français et les autres langues de communication. In M. Blancpain and A. Rebouillet (eds) *Une Langue: Le français aujourd'hui dans le monde.* Paris: Hachette.

House of Commons Home Affairs Committee (1990) *Seventh Report: Practical Police Co-operation in the European Community.* London: HMSO.

— (1991a) *First Report: Fire Safety and Policing the Channel Tunnel: Vol.I: Report Together with the Proceedings of the Committee.* London: HMSO.

— (1991b) *First Report: Fire, Safety and Policing of the Channel Tunnel: Vol.II, Minutes of Evidence and Appendices.* London: HMSO.

Hughes, R. (1988) *The Fatal Shore.* London: Pan Books.

Ingleton, R. (1992) *Dictionary of Police and Criminal Law.* Amsterdam: Elsevier

Irving, B.L. and McKenzie, I.K. (1989) *Police Interrogation: The Effects of the Police & Criminal Evidence Act, 1984.* London: The Police Foundation.

James, C.V. (1978) Foreign languages in the school curriculum. *Foreign Languages in Education.* London, NCLE Papers and Reports 1.

Jenkins, C. (1980) *Language Links: The European Family of Languages.* London: Harrap.

Kendall, R. (1992) Kendall calls for caution on Europol. Report in *Police Review* 31 January, 188.

Kent County Constabulary (1992) Radio voice tuned to right wave-length. *The New Relay* (Kent police newspaper), No.17, 3.

Kingscott, G. (1991) The Canadian language question. *Language International* 3 (3), 23–4.

Koster, C.J. (1991) Is the knowledge of languages in the Netherlands good enough for Europe 1992? *Language International* 3 (4), 5.

Littlewood, W. (1984) *Foreign and Second Language Learning.* Cambridge: Cambridge University Press.

Lustgarten, L. (1986) *The Governance of the Police.* London: Sweet and Maxwell.

MacNamara, J. (1967) The bilingual's linguistic performance. *The Journal of Social Issues* 23, 58–77.

McKenzie, I.K. and Gallagher, G.P. (1989) *Behind the Uniform: Policing in Britain and America*. Hemel Hempstead: Harvester Wheatsheaf.

Mitchell, B. and Robinson, F.C. (1964) *A Guide to Old English*. Oxford: Basil Blackwell.

Munro, S.M. (1987) Bilingualism in Wales. In S. Abudarham (ed.) *Bilingualism and the Bilingual*. Windsor: NFER-Nelson.

Owen, R. and Dynes, M. (1989) *The Times Guide to 1992*. London: Times Books Ltd.

Pandit, P.B. (1989) Perspectives on sociolinguistics in India. In W.C. McCormack and S.A. Wurm (eds) *Language and Society: Anthropological Issues* (pp. 171–82). The Hague/Paris/New York: Mouton.

Police Federation (1992) Into Europe. *Police* February, 28.

Price, G. (1984) *The Languages of Britain*. London: Edward Arnold.

Prince of Wales (H.R.H.) (1990) Address to the Royal Society of Arts. Reported in *The Linguist* 29 (5), 149.

Reenen, Van, P. (1989) Policing Europe after 1992: Co-operation and competition. *European Affairs* Summer, 45.

Reeves, N. (1989) Languages, the barrier no EC directive can eliminate. *The Linguist* 28 (1), 2–7.

Reiner, R. (1982) Who are the police? *Political Quarterly* 53.2.

— (1985) *The Politics of the Police*. Hemel Hempstead: Harvester Wheatsheaf.

Robson, C. (1973) *Experiment, Design and Statistics in Psychology*. London: Penguin Books.

Sheppard, C. (1992) Language and the law. *Police Review* 3 January, 33.

Skolnick, J. (1969) *The Politics of Protest*. New York: Ballantine.

— (1972) *Changing Conceptions of the Police*. Chicago: Encyclopaedia Britannica.

Spencer, C. (1989) Linguistic chauvinism. Summarised in *Language International* 1 (4), 17.

Swaan, de, A. (1991) Notes on the emerging global language system: Regional, national and supranational. In *Media, Culture and Society*. Vol. 13. London/ Newbury Park/New Delhi: Sage.

Tamaron, The Marquess of (1992) Talking the same language. *The European* 16/19 July, 1992.

Tomlins, J. (1991) Speak French, says Mitterand, or bid adieu to your job. *Daily Mail* 22 November.

Trofimov, Y. (1992) A language of separation. *The European* 31.1.1992.

Watson, R. (1992) Home affairs and justice. *The European* 23.7.1992.

Weber, G. (1990) The end: Scattered thoughts on the decline and fall of languages. *Language International* 2 (5), 5–13.

Westgate, D. (1989) French: First among equals. In D. Phillips (ed.) *Which Language*. London: Hodder & Stoughton.

Wickland, N. (1989) Executive/linguist or linguist/executive? *The Linguist* 28 (6), 210–11.

Will, I. (1990) A service built on sinking sand. *Police Review* 14 September, 1854–6.

Wolfson College (1989) PoliceSpeak: The Channel Tunnel Communications Project. Unpublished report to the Kent County Constabulary.

— (1992) PoliceSpeak Report: Phase II. Unpublished report to the Kent County Constabulary.

Index